PENGUIN

ARKANA

The Power of the Pendulum

T. C. Lethbridge, who died in 1971, was an archaeologist, psychic researcher, dowser, explorer. He was for thirty years Director of Excavations for the Cambridge Antiquarian Society and for the University Museum of Archaeology and Ethnology. He was on three Arctic expeditions, several Hebridean exploratory expeditions and two voyages to the Baltic in square-rigged sailing ships. He was also, as Colin Wilson wrote, 'one of the most remarkable and original minds in parapsychology'.

The Power of the Pendulum

T. C. Lethbridge

ARKANA
PENGUIN BOOKS

ARKANA

Published by the Penguin Group
Penguin Books Ltd, 27 Wrights Lane, London W8 5TZ, England
Penguin Books USA Inc., 375 Hudson Street, New York, New York 10014, USA
Penguin Books Australia Ltd, Ringwood, Victoria, Australia
Penguin Books Canada Ltd, 10 Alcorn Avenue, Toronto, Ontario, Canada M4V 3B2
Penguin Books (NZ) Ltd, 182–190 Wairau Road, Auckland 10, New Zealand

Penguin Books Ltd, Registered Offices: Harmondsworth, Middlesex, England

First published in the USA by Routledge & Kegan Paul 1976
Published in Great Britain by Arkana 1984
10 9 8 7 6 5 4

Printed in England by Clays Ltd, St Ives plc

Contents

Figures

Foreword by
Colin Wilson

I feel that it is largely my own fault that I missed the pleasure—and profit—of knowing T. C. Lethbridge. He moved to Devon in 1957, the same year that I moved to Cornwall; so until his death in 1971, we were living within a hundred miles of one another. Moreover, in 1965, I picked up a copy of his book, *Witches: Investigating an Ancient Religion*, and observed opposite the title page that he had written a book called *Ghost and Ghoul*. Two years later, I was commissioned by an American publisher to write a book on 'the occult', and settled down to research the subject. I actually quoted *Witches* in the finished book—the anecdote on p.15, in which he was led, blindfolded, around the cliffs on Lundy Island, holding a dowsing rod, and accurately detected the position of every one of its buried volcanic dykes. Not long after the book appeared, a correspondent asked me why I didn't contact Lethbridge, since he lived so close; accordingly, I packed up a copy of *The Occult* and sent it to him, together with a letter introducing myself. It was his wife, Mina, who replied, telling me that he had died recently. It was only then, lazily and belatedly, that I bought a copy of *Ghost and Ghoul*, and realised with astonishment—and chagrin—that here was a completely new and original theory about the nature of ghosts, which ought to have been discussed at length in my book. I made a kind of belated apology by dedicating my book *Strange Powers*, to Lethbridge and his wife Mina. Since then, I have read all his books, with a growing sense of frustration at the missed opportunity. Now, in introducing his last book, I can at least pay tribute to a man who seems to me to be one of the most remarkable and original minds in parapsychology.

Curiously enough, this interest developed only after the Lethbridges moved to Branscombe, in Devon. Before that, Lethbridge had spent most of his adult life in Cambridge— where he was Keeper of Anglo-Saxon Antiquities at the University Museum of Archaeology and Ethnology. (It was a purely 'honorary' post, but Lethbridge was glad of the independence; he disliked university 'trade unionism' and the need for academic respectability.) Born in 1901, he came to Cambridge soon after the First World War as a student, and it remained his base for the next thirty-five years or so (with the exception of an eighteen-month break in the mid-1940s, when he and Mina, newly married, tried to become cattle farmers on an island off the west coast of Scotland). His attitude to Cambridge seems to have been ambivalent; he left there in 1944 because he was sick of it, but returned because he missed it. By 1957—when *Gogmagog* appeared—the love affair with Cambridge was definitely over; he felt the place was becoming too brash and noisy, and the hostile reception given to *Gogmagog* by archaeological colleagues did nothing to strengthen his attachment. Mina—whose family is from Devon—located Hole House, a fourteenth-century house, with attached cottage, near Branscombe, and felt that this was the place they had always been looking for. She was right; they were exceptionally happy there.

Up to this time, Lethbridge's major works were *Merlin's Island* (1948), *Herdsmen and Hermits* (1950), *The Painted Men* (1954) and *Gogmagog*; there are also a number of smaller works on boats including *Boats and Boatmen* (1952) and *Coastwide Craft* (1952). Nothing is more obvious than that Lethbridge thoroughly enjoyed writing. It was probably fortunate that he came to it so late. He had always been a 'loner', whose twin loves were archaeology and the sea. By the time he was in his mid-forties, this independence of mind was well developed and was expressed in a style that was easy, casual and personal. *Merlin's Island* begins by explaining that the friends whose help he acknowledges are in no way responsible for the 'damnable heresies' contained in its pages. (I am not sufficiently well versed in Anglo-Saxon history to know what these are.) And in a foreword to *Herdsmen and Hermits*, T. D. Kendrick, Director of the British Museum, comments with a kind of reluctant admiration: 'It is here that his opinions, on such subjects, for instance, as the early voyages in northern waters, become almost aggressively memorable, even when one has decided not to believe in them. "This pretty picture may be absolutely incorrect", he remarks cheerfully when talking of the broch people . . .'

Gogmagog: The Buried Gods is the story of Lethbridge's search for a giant figure cut into the turf near Cambridge, and it includes a number of startling theories—such as that Druidism and Brahmanism had a common origin at some time in the remote past. It is possible to understand why it aroused academic hostility. To begin with, a number of references to his friend and colleague Margaret Murray make it clear that he accepts her basic theory, advanced in *The God of the Witches*, that 'witchcraft' is an ancient nature religion based on the worship of the moon goddess Diana. The theory has always had many supporters, and as many bitter opponents, who regard it as little better than imaginative fiction. Margaret Murray enjoyed the dismay she caused; she even enjoyed teasing her academic colleagues until they were speechless with rage. Lethbridge's book concludes that the ancient religion of prehistoric England was the worship of the earth mother, Magog (who is identified with the moon) and her husband Gog, the sun, and his views could be interpreted as powerful support for Margaret Murray's theories of 'wicca'. As I re-read the book, I can see why it would enrage academic historians; what is astonishing is that a member of an academic community—and keeper of a university museum—could write with such breezy independence of mind and such a lack of the usual conditional clauses.

If the attacks hastened Lethbridge's decision to leave Cambridge, then we should thank his hostile colleagues. The independence allowed his mind to return to a subject that had always interested him: the hidden powers of the mind. His mother had been fascinated by the subject of fortune telling and in the days of his first marriage Lethbridge himself had taken an interest in the powers of a clairvoyant who was able to 'see' scenes from the past. Lethbridge had seen a ghost in his undergraduate days at Cambridge—I shall refer to this again in a moment—and had also discovered, at a fairly early stage, that he was a good dowser.

Now, at Branscombe, they made the acquaintance of an elderly lady who was wholly immersed in 'occult' subjects. She talked to them about pendulums, pentagrams and related matters. She was also, apparently, able to 'project her astral body', and wander around and visit her acquaintances at night, as he tells in this present book (and also in *The Legend of the Sons of God*). Lethbridge apparently tried his skill with a pendulum, and discovered that it worked. The pendulum is used in much the same way as the divining rod but can give far more information. Not only will it swing in a circle over some buried object (say, a silver spoon) but can also give precise information on the age of the buried object. It can 'answer questions'—which leads Lethbridge to conclude that it actually serves as some form of contact between a part of the mind that already knows these things, and our limited everyday consciousness. I personally have no doubt whatever that certain minds can perceive all kinds of things that are hidden from the rest of us. I spent two days in Utrecht making a television documentary about the 'paragnost' Gerard Croiset. Like some freak television set, Croiset's mind picks up spontaneous 'pictures' of other times and other places. For example, he might be handed a wrapped parcel connected with an unsolved murder case, and say: 'This contains a cigarette box and a potato sack. The box came from the house of one of two brothers who murdered a teenage girl in a cow barn, and the sack was used to wrap her body . . . .' Croiset is also able to 'see' the future; in many cases of drowning, he has been able to say: 'The body will float to the surface next Tuesday morning in the vicinity of the maritime museum in the Hague . . .', and has been proved correct. Croiset's everyday consciousness is apparently able to have direct contact with this 'other mind'—perhaps the 'Superconscious'—that knows such things. Lethbridge believes that, for at least one third of mankind (perhaps more), the pendulum can produce the same kind of results, although with less detail.

The experience of using the pendulum, and the sense of freedom from academic restraints, apparently decided Lethbridge to write a book about 'occult' topics. The result was *Ghost and Ghoul*, a book I now heartily wish I had read when it appeared in 1961. In this book, Lethbridge advances the interesting theory that many 'ghosts'—perhaps the majority—are simply a form of 'tape recording'. This line of thought developed from his experience with pendulums. He had established, to his own satisfaction, that material things retain the impress of events in which they have been involved. A sling stone used in a battle two thousand years ago still gives a reading for 'anger' when a 40 inch pendulum is suspended above it. A paragnost like Croiset might well receive actual impressions of the battle as he held the stone. Is it not possible that many 'ghosts' are 'recordings' that are played back accidentally when the right observer comes along? The same thing seems to be true of 'ghouls', or the 'nasty feeling' that can be experienced in certain places. Lethbridge has a fascinating story, dating back to 1924, of a ghoul he encountered in a chorister's school in a cathedral close. He and a friend walked into the spot at the bottom of the stairs and experienced a 'wall of icy cold', imbued with a feeling of misery. When they stepped towards it, the 'ghoul' retreated up the stairs. They followed it step by step up to the roof, wondering if it would suddenly materialise and confront them; instead, it reappeared behind them, and they drove it back downstairs to the hall. This 'ghoul', Lethbridge thought, had been projected from the subconscious mind of some person who was afraid of a ghost that was reputed to haunt the end room in the corridor.

A comparison of *Ghost and Ghoul* and the slightly later *Ghost and Divining Rod* (1963) enables us to see the way in which Lethbridge's theories developed. (The book that came in between these two was *Witches*, but since this deals mainly with Margaret Murray—type theories of witchcraft, it need not concern us here.) In the earlier book, he had described seeing the ghost of a woman of about seventy in a garden near Hole House, and advanced the theory that she was a 'projection' of somebody's mind. Now, in *Ghost and Divining Rod*, he draws a further conclusion from something he had already noticed in the earlier book: that an underground stream ran under the lane where he was standing, imparting to the atmosphere above it a 'tingly' feeling. He also mentions a 'ghoul' which both he and his wife experienced on Ladram beach, at a spot where a stream ran into the sea. Could the 'electromagnetic field' of the water be somehow to blame—that same 'field' that produces the response in the dowsing rod? Is it possible that such fields can receive the impress of an emotion, as the sling stone received the impress of anger, and transmit it later to someone who stands on the same spot? He invents the term 'naiad field' for the electromagnetic field of water, and advances the suggestion that mountains and open spaces (like deserts) may also have their own individual fields.

Throughout the nine 'occult' books (beginning with *Gogmagog* and ending with the present volume), Lethbridge's thought is always changing and expanding. Sometimes he changes his mind completely; more often, he modifies a theory advanced in an earlier volume. None of the books attempts to present a complete 'system' of ideas; a theme that is only mentioned in one may be developed in another. (For example, the theme of precognition and dreaming is briefly mentioned in *Ghost and Ghoul*, to be fully developed in the present volume.) The final impression is of a brilliant, intuitive intelligence that never ceases to develop.

My own impression is that with the book called *ESP: Beyond Time and Distance* (1965), Lethbridge entered a new phase of his investigation. In the preface, he describes an incident that occurred on one of his early journeys of exploration to Greenland; chasing a wounded bear, he suddenly fell through a hole in the ice and found himself floundering in icy water. Now, he says, something of a similar nature has happened to me again: 'I seem o have suddenly fallen through into [a world] where there are more dimensions.' I feel that, up to this point, he had thought of himself basically as an archaeologist and naturalist who was pursuing a rather interesting sideline. Now it seems as if he has suddenly recognised that what he is 'on to' may be more important than any of his work as an archaeologist. The books take on a new force and direction; now he experiments non-stop with the pendulum, and makes all kind of interesting discoveries. For example, a casual remark by his wife—about why some trees are considered 'unlucky'—led him to try studying various types of wood with the pendulum. Elder—a traditionally unlucky tree—gave a reaction for maleness and repulsion, while rowan—regarded as a protection against magic spells—gave a reaction for femaleness and attraction. One remembers Tolkien's hostile trees in *The Lord of the Rings*, and Robert Graves' long investigations into the ancient tree worship of the Druids. It becomes possible to see what Lethbridge meant by saying he felt as if he had stumbled into another world. Like Graves, he believes that 'earlier men knew far more about all this than we know today'. But Graves also believed that these early men possessed another *kind* of knowledge than we possess today. Our knowledge is mostly intellectual, a 'daylight' knowledge, which Graves associates with the sun; there is another kind of intuitive knowledge, a 'lunar' knowledge, symbolised by the White Moon Goddess herself.

This seems to me to be one of the most exciting things about Lethbridge. He is always stumbling on important insights. Sometimes he follows them up; sometimes he merely mentions them in passing. I have heard his books criticised on the grounds that they are repetitive and inconclusive. But this is necessarily so. They are a kind of working journal into which he poured his fresh discoveries and insights year by year; if they are chaotic, they share that fault with the notebooks of Leonardo and the daily journals of every important discoverer. It is fortunate for us that Lethbridge decided to write down his discoveries piecemeal in seven or eight small books, rather than storing them up for some large definitive work; the book might never have been written, and the notes would still be unpublished.

But it was in the next book, *A Step in the Dark*, that Lethbridge first stated what may be his major discovery. In *ESP*, he had noted that the pendulum 'rate' for death seems to be 40 inches, and that dead objects also respond to 20 inches; which led him to speculate that 40 inches may 'represent life force on a higher plane'. All earthly objects, including such ideas as danger and time, have rates between 0 and 40. But by extending the pendulum beyond 40—the death rate—Lethbridge discovered that the pendulum responds once again—the new length being its 'earthly' rate, *plus* 40. (I.e. the rate for carbon is 12, and it can also be detected at 52.) But the pendulum now swings over a 'false position' to one side of the object. Lethbridge concludes that there is another realm or dimension in which things also exist—beyond death. Moreover, if the pendulum is extended yet another 40 inches, the same thing happens all over again. But the pendulum gives no rate for 'time' on the second level, as if this realm is somehow timeless; after that, on higher levels, time comes back again. Readers may find this short exposition bewildering, but Lethbridge develops the whole idea further in the present book, and so I can refer them to him.

In short, Lethbridge came to suspect that the pendulum is revealing a realm on the other side of death, perhaps several. Its 'energy rates' seem to be higher than ours, according to the pendulum. Oddly enough, the curious researches of Dr Constantin Raudive on the 'ghost voices' that sometimes appear on magnetic tape seem to point to the same conclusion; these voices seem to be about twice as fast as earthly speech. (Anyone who wants to pursue this point should read Raudive's book *Breakthrough*, and listen to the record that goes with it.) I may also refer to the theories of my friend Dr David Foster, author of *The Intelligent Universe*; Foster is a cybernetician, but has become convinced that the genes of living creatures could only be 'coded' by higher energies than exist on earth—possibly some form of cosmic rays. (I have summarised his idea in the introduction to *The Occult*.) Lethbridge himself was, from the beginning, much preoccupied with this whole problem of Darwinian evolution—with the question: Could living creatures have evolved through a *mechanical* system? His answer—predictably in the negative—is set out most fully in *The Monkey's Tail* (1969), the book that followed *A Step in the Dark*.

If I needed further evidence that Lethbridge possessed intuitive genius of a high order, it would be provided by his last published book, *The Legend of the Sons of God* (which appeared posthumously). In 1968, a German publisher had brought out a book called *Memory of the Future*, which came out in England in 1969 as *Chariots of the Gods?*. It made its author, Erich von Däniken, a rich man. But by this time Lethbridge was already at work on *The Legend of the Sons of God*, which looks as if he had read and digested Däniken. (In fact, as he mentions in his preface to *Legend*, he knew nothing of Däniken until a friend sent him the book just as his wife was finishing the typing of *Legend*.) For, like Däniken, Lethbridge is preoccupied with the question of the great stone megaliths like Stonehenge—or the stone circle called the Merry Maidens, in Cornwall. When he tested the Merry Maidens with a pendulum, the reaction was so powerful that the pendulum described a circle that was almost horizontal to the ground. He concluded that some great force is stored in these stones. His arguments led him to the conclusion that the great stone megaliths could have been erected as guides to descending aircraft—a kind of 'landing light'. But if beings landed on our earth as long ago as 2000 BC, then they must have been from another planet, perhaps another galaxy . . . . Why are there so many legends of 'sons of god' in ancient literature—angels who came down to earth and mated with human beings?

The energy stored in these stones—and probably induced by frenzied religious dances—was probably a form of 'bio-energy', Lethbridge believes. Presumably the spacemen who visited our earth understood how to utilise this energy. It seems a pity that Lethbridge never came across the interesting ideas of John Michell and his fellow 'ley hunters', who believe that the straight tracks that can be traced on Ordnance Survey maps—ancient bridle paths—joined spots on the earth's surface in which this bio-energy reached a high level—sacred places like Glastonbury and Stonehenge. I do not know what he would have thought of the theory but I am convinced that he would have taken it seriously.

This whole subject is too big to be discussed here. Lethbridge would obviously have developed his ideas on the 'sons of god' if he had lived, and he would probably have done so more skilfully and plausibly than Däniken, whose excesses have led many people to dismiss the whole thing as pure fantasy. I myself was inclined to take that view after reading Däniken; it was Lethbridge's book that caused me to change my mind.

I should add that I have also tried dowsing at the Merry Maidens and, to my amazement, it worked. I say to my amazement because on the only occasion when I had tried dowsing before—in my own back garden—nothing happened, although my wife got a strong reaction. At the Merry Maidens, a friend, Gaston de St Pierre, showed me how to hold the rod; and as I moved beyond the limit of the circle of stones, it shot up until it was almost vertical. Clearly, it was not responding to water, for the 'line of power' runs around the Merry Maidens in a circle, about two feet beyond the stones, and there is unlikely to be a circular underground stream. The centre of the circle also gives a powerful reaction. The day was too windy to try a pendulum; but I am inclined to doubt whether it would work for me. I have tried it in the house, without result. (Again, my wife does it very well.) Lethbridge suggests that people with a strong sexual impulse may be poor at dowsing, and this may explain it; anyone who has read my books will have noted the basic sexual theme that runs through them.

As to the matter of the megaliths, I happened to raise this question with the economist E. F. Schumacher shortly after finishing Lethbridge's book. Without prompting, he remarked that he had just returned from an extensive tour of the Middle East, in which he had seen many ancient buildings and tombs with their massive stone blocks, and that he found it inconceivable that the explanation of these blocks could be as simple as the academic archaeologists insist. This was my own feeling when I visited the ruins at Baalbek in 1974, and looked at giant carved blocks that must have taken years to shape and move into place.

I believe that if Lethbridge had lived a year or two longer, he would have become something of a cult figure. (As it is, admirers have raised the idea of starting a Tom Lethbridge Society.) The 'occult revival' began in the early 1960s in France, and by the mid-1960s it had spread all over the world. This may explain why Lethbridge's publishers encouraged him to go on producing an average of a book every eighteen months throughout the 1960s. Some of the experts believed that the 'craze' would be over by the early 1970s; but at this moment, there is no sign of it; on the contrary, it seems to be gathering momentum. English and American publishers reprint books that have been out of print for seventy years (when the last 'occult revival' ground to a halt), and the paperback houses send out a steady stream of popular books on witchcraft, black magic, astral travel and astrology. Hardly any of these books have anything new to say, although some of them—like Lyall Watson's *Supernature*—are important summaries of what modern science thinks of the 'paranormal'. Lethbridge's books stand out for their clarity, originality, and sheer literary quality. He was a born writer. He was also the sort of person who would, as he became known to a wider public, have drawn disciples and followers. With a figure like G. K. Chesterton's, he also had some of his personal qualities: kindliness, a child-like humour, and a mind that bubbled with ideas like a glass of champagne. To my mind, these personal qualities emerge most clearly in his unpublished autobiography, one of the most delightful works of its kind I have read since Yeats's. But they can also be found in this present volume—which is, in some ways, one of his most ambitious books. His aim is to review the whole question of whether the world can be described in terms of scientific materialism, or whether something closer to the religious view is correct. Lethbridge is not religious in the ordinary sense—his wife seemed to think he was probably an agnostic. But a man who believes he has accidentally stumbled on a way of establishing that there are other realms of reality beyond this one, and that the 'soul' is probably immortal, has more in common with the religious man than with the sceptic. In fact, Lethbridge was inclined to believe that such distinctions are unnecessary. 'What is magic today will be science tomorrow', he says in one of his books. And this remark could be quoted on the title page of all his books; it catches their essential spirit.

One of these days, some enterprising publisher will gather together all Tom Lethbridge's 'occult' books between two covers—it would not be unmanageably large. When that

happens, I think we shall recognise that he is a classic: not just
of parapsychology, but of English Literature.

Introduction

At the time of his death my husband, Tom Lethbridge, had just finished writing the manuscript of this book. He had no chance of going through it and re-arranging it in any way.

Due to the encouragement of his friends, I decided I would try and get it in shape. I was very anxious to do this as the book seemed to contain a good summing up of his theories and ideas. Also, as we always worked as a team, I felt I was the only person who could really do the job. I have no experience of editing and the task was daunting; but for all our friends and for Tom's memory I was determined to do my best. I hope that it has finally turned out more or less as he would have wished.

Without the help, advice and encouragement of our cousins, Bridget and Peter Acland, I doubt if I would have had the confidence to fight on after various rebuffs from others at my original attempt. Peter spent a very long time reading the manuscript, both with me and by himself. I can never thank him enough for all he did. If the book does emerge finally, it will be entirely due to his kindness, help, shrewd judgment and common sense.

M.L.

1 Our Great Dilemma

Perhaps I could have called this book 'Our Great Problem' or, better still, refrained from writing it at all. The word 'dilemma' is really the right one, for it implies that whatever path we choose, we are liable to risk being hurt. Not only have we to try to solve a problem; but we have then to arrange our subsequent actions in accordance with this solution.

The problem is this: do we live a planned life in a created universe; or is the whole thing a matter of chance? It must be one or the other. Either the ingredients for life were deliberately prepared for it, or it all happened by accident.

This is where the horns of the dilemma come in, for if we decide that it was deliberately prepared, we are clearly under an obligation to make the best of it, employing as a guide an indefinable element known as 'conscience'. If we decide it is all chance, then there is no point in acting in any other way than that which appears to offer us the most pleasure. It is a matter of observed fact that either course may land us on one or other of the dilemma's sharp horns.

Somewhere, I suppose, there is an ancient word picture, or even a drawing, of a dilemma; but it does not happen to be familiar to me. Perhaps the nearest ancient drawing of this kind of thing is the well-known Dark Ages one in the Vienna Gospels of a devil appearing to St Cuthbert, but this apparition has no horns and is not worth illustrating here. We do not know how a dilemma appeared to those who invented the term for use in logic long ago. I imagine it as a small, dark, shaggy, bull-like creature, with what the Americans call a 'mean' expression in its little, red, piggy eyes, and with sharp, forward-curving horns.

For thousands of years there appears to have been no question of our problem ever arising. In general man, according to Christian teaching, may have been heathen; but he did believe in superior entities who had created the Universe, the earth, the animals and mankind itself. Christianity, Sufi, Buddhism, Brahmanism, Muhammadism and the rest were really just sects of one belief in a Universal Creator. The dogmas which arose and the wars between conflicting ideas were about relatively small matters compared with that which has come upon us now. The bulk of Western man today, if he can be bothered to think about it at all, favours the idea that everything happens by chance. It is no good for professionals of religion to tell their flock that they must have faith. The flock just has not got it and it disregards most of the dogma. They ask how God can possibly be Love when such frightful things happen to them. I should be inclined to this belief myself, had not another possible explanation come my way. Since it has come, it is obviously a matter of duty to set it out for others to examine and think about. My ideas may well be wrong; but I do not think that they can be so conflicting with observed fact as is the theory of chance.

As a matter of interest, variants of ideas like mine are held by many people all over the world; but relatively few are prepared to write things which can lead others to regard them as crazy. It is perfectly fair. Many regard Darwinian Evolutionists as too simple to be allowed loose on humanity; but few dare to put this on paper. A theory has become a dogma and this is kept alive by faith. To shift a dogma of this kind may take hundreds of years. Millions of children have been taught that all living animals have evolved from lumps of jelly in the sea, and why should they doubt it? Actually the idea is apparently already out of date and discarded; but the belief in it will go on. The amoeba theory will take years to replace, for it has become a kind of religious belief. What was Voltaire's remark on this kind of thing? I forget the exact words but translated they went something like this: 'Religion is a series of inhibitions, which prevents a man from making full use of his intelligence.' Of course this is only true of dogma. Belief in Darwinian Evolution has reached this dogma stage. Darwin did not wish it but his enthusiastic followers overrode him. It is very difficult now even to discuss the possibility that it might be wrong. It is on this Evolution theory, which is not even supported by the record of fossils in the more ancient rocks, that the whole idea of the development of the Universe by Chance rests. The alternative is that the Universe was deliberately planned and created by an entity known as God. This cannot be proved either. Both beliefs are kept going by faith. Is there any way of finding out which idea is the more probable? For it is widely apparent that there is something wrong with the leadership of both ways of thinking.

There is another method of trying to solve our dilemma, which is the one we will try to use in this book. If it could be satisfactorily demonstrated, both the other ideas could be combined. There would no longer be a gulf between science and religion; although this closing of the gap would certainly not be popular with some of the professionals of both groups. I do not know whether I can present the facts in a readable manner and I know that I am certainly not the proper person to make the attempt; but, since nobody else appears to be doing so, I am prepared to try, even if it earns me nothing but contempt. At least I have spent a dozen years in practical efforts to find out the answer.

It is easy to say to oneself that there are these two views and it really does not matter very much which one is right. What can we do about it anyway? But it does matter, because, if the dogma of chance is established, there is nothing to prevent a rule of complete selfishness and greed overwhelming the world. The most ruthless people will come to the top and reign as dictators. The remainder will do what they are told to do. The great example of this is Russia, where the patron saint, Karl Marx, built up his theory on that of Darwin. But we have not sunk as low as this yet and are hardly likely to accept as a paragon of virtue a man who was habitually hit over the head by his wife with a rolling pin. Yet the theory does corrupt and in the hands of clever men can cause great damage by its influence.

That in brief is one side of the picture. The other is of the church's long rearguard action. Now and then attempts are made to update the theories which first took root well over a thousand years ago. The difficulty appears to be that, while the congregation is desperately willing to know whether there is such a thing as God, their teachers spend their time in telling them what God wants them to do. Naturally enough the congregation would like to know how they came by this knowledge. They must have faith, they are told. Where do you obtain this commodity? God is Love they are told, and on looking about they can see very little sign of it.

To the outside observer neither faith seems to be correct. Somewhere between the two, or perhaps entirely independent of either, there must be a third. Although it may seem a very impertinent quest, I see no valid reason why we should not try to find it. We are provided with a thinking mechanism. Why not use it?

2   Time, Mind and Dreams

On 28 July 1923, at 1 a.m., I was asleep in my bunk in the forehold of the Norwegian sealer, *Heimen*. Suddenly there was a series of crashes and creaking of the ship's timbers. With me in the forehold slept the members of a small Cambridge expedition on the way to East Greenland. We were held up in very thick pack-ice, which some believe to be the heaviest in the world.

When the crashes began we were quickly out of our bunks and up the ladder to the deck. Here was a somewhat grim sight. The ship was caught between two revolving ice fields, each perhaps half a mile in extent. Blocks of pack-ice were already heaped at her sides almost level with the bridge. It was realised at once that the vessel might be crushed at any minute and had to be abandoned instantly. We hurried below and packed our gear; expecting to see tongues of ice coming through the planking while we did so. Everything was carried up on to the nearest ice field and, as daylight broadened, stock was taken of the situation.

By the terms of the charter the Norwegian crew of the sealer should have had enough stores to last the winter in case we were forced to stay in Greenland by the ice. Actually the Norwegians had nothing but a couple of bags of potatoes! We had plenty of stores for ourselves, but not enough to feed the whole ship's complement. Although Greenland was close—only about thirty miles away—it was useless to go there (to a barren wilderness) unless there was enough for us to eat. The only alternative was to get out of the pack-ice in the ship's hunting boats and then make a 300 mile open voyage in them to Iceland.

The ship was not crushed. By what seemed a miracle, a ton of ice had passed completely beneath her keel and took the pressure off her against the other ice field. All day we sat about on the ice and presently the fields slowly rolled apart. The ship was left propped up on a spur and, by dint of considerable labour, we eventually refloated her.

The thing which made the most impression on me during this unimportant incident was the speed at which everything in the sequence of events developed. One moment we were snug and comfortable in our bunks; the next we were survivors from a wreck. For weeks, time had just been ticking slowly along; now it went by like a mill-race. Of course the clock time remained steady; but what one might perhaps call 'Mental' time had changed completely. This I hope to show later is a matter of great importance.

The question of the meaning of Time is going to figure largely in this investigation, for it appears to be a key, which may unlock many boxes of secrets. Time, as we know it in daily life, is just a convenience for the observation of sequences of events. It is not the time which interests us but the sequence. It is obvious that there is no such thing as a fixed time scale for all living things. Time to a blue tit is quite different from time to an oak tree and to us. It is no more than the chopping up into portions of the period taken by the earth to revolve on its own axis. In fact time is one of these difficult words with many different meanings. There is no such thing as a fixed universal scale. Even to us the divisions of our arbitrary time scale can pass at very differing speeds. I was once caught under the sail of a capsized boat. It seemed a month before I struggled free; but it can hardly have been half a minute. Our respectable time scale does not really work and what is happening in the observer's mind need not have any relation to it at all. Two people may travel to America by the same plane. For each the same number of divisions of the scale are occupied by the journey; but for one, who wants to get there in a desperate hurry, the time will drag and seem much longer than it does to the other, who does not wish to go there at all.

Right at the beginning we seem to have fallen on one of the horns of the dilemma and it is called Time. It is a horn, because the scientist gives one meaning to it and the theologian another. The scientist thinks, with some reason, that he can date the creation (or should I say formation?) of the world within a given number of millions of years. From that point he believes that everything evolved by chance. The strict theologian, on the other hand, used to believe that the universe was created by God in six days and that it was God Himself who created all its fauna and flora. Actually there is enough resemblance between the second theory and the findings of geology (if we accept that in the eyes of God a thousand years are but as yesterday) to suggest that someone, a very long time ago, knew more about the origin of species than anyone knew again for thousands of years. This is not unusual. Here and there about the world, fragments of old beliefs still remain, which look very much like survivals from an age of considerable learning and experiment.

In my lifetime there has only been one man who could really bring home to people the importance of the study of Time, for he saw that it carried with it the answer to whether there was a plan in life and whether it continued beyond the point which we call death. Dunne was no ivory tower contemplative, but a practical man, who could design machines, which would fly at a time when few others could get them to leave the ground. When his first book, *An Experiment with Time*, came out, it caused the greatest interest and thrill all over the world.

Dunne's work can be divided into two parts. The first consists of practical observation of his own dreams and many of us can testify that it is, as one might expect, entirely accurate. The second part was based on mathematical theory and for this there was not at the time the information available to make it a success. The first part was devastating, for it showed clearly that, during sleep, the human mind could remember events which had not yet happened in earth time. Of course it was vital for this to be the subject of intense theological investigation. If the future could be shown to exist, what happened to the doctrine of free will? There may have been some fluttering in the ecclesiastical dovecotes but if any eggs were laid I have not seen them. It was probably thought better to ignore Dunne and hope that in a short time his bombshell would be forgotten. People have not forgotten.

The other horn of the dilemma prodded Dunne's mathematics and, as there the information was not complete, flaws were thought to have been found in the reasoning. So wiseacres nodded their heads when Dunne was mentioned and said: 'So-and-so has shown that his mathematics were wrong.' However, this is not the point and it would have been better if the theory had not been included in the book at all. Many people now realise that future memories exist in dreams.

In brief, Dunne's theory was that every person was built up of a series of observers, each watching the actions of the one in front. The only observer who ever died was the first one. The others continued to observe.

It seems now that, though there may be a series of observers, each is not a replica of the preceding one. They appear to become more learned and intelligent in succession. The point here is that Dunne had apparently altered our conception of time, but the thinking world was too lazy to take it seriously. I am kind in calling inaction 'lazy', for it is obvious that many vested interests were involved also. The Church might have to rethink its explanation of the doctrine of free will.

Accustomed as scientists were to dealing with one world in which they need only trouble with what could be weighed and measured, how were they to regard memory, which they could not measure? And a world of sleep was beyond their terms of reference. There must have been a considerable number of people on both sides who felt guilty about all this. But the younger ones would realise that their bread and butter was at risk if they admitted taking an interest in such outrageous matters. And so, as the years went by, the moss grew over Dunne and his quite shattering discoveries. He himself fully appreciated that there was hope for millions in what he had made known, but one man can of himself do little, especially when he cannot have been quite confident that he had found the right solution. Now, more than a generation later, the dilemma is still with us, though it may have had some setbacks, for scientists (especially physicists) are no longer sure where their subject is leading them. The ecclesiastics too are having their difficulties, with revolts against ancient dogma breaking out at times. But the solution, which might have come from Dunne's work, is still to be found and to most of humanity must appear as remote as ever.

The one vital question, which mankind wants to know, is whether his personality, individuality, or whatever you like to call 'himself', is extinguished at death. Solve this and then all the exploits of atom splitters and astronauts are simply light entertainment.

To get any bearing on this subject, it is necessary to enter a realm where the individual has to work out his own answers. He simply cannot find all he wants in someone else's book. It is also a country in which nothing can be weighed and measured, nothing proved to the satisfaction of the earth-bound scientist. In fact the investigator has to develop his own faith with which to satisfy himself. The lazy-minded man can get nowhere.

It must have been thirty years ago that I first read *An Experiment with Time*. I was interested but, being busy with archaeological matters, did no more than try a few dreams to see whether there was anything in the theory that they sometimes contained future memories. Having experienced one or two, which seemed to confirm Dunne's contention, I forgot all about the matter and returned to my own work, which in itself gave plenty of mental exercise to anybody.

After moving from Cambridge to Devon in 1957, my wife and I became involved in parapsychology, that is the study of what is generally known as the occult. The term is rather ponderous and occult is only occult (i.e. hidden) as long as it is not understood. As far as we are concerned the occult is far less hidden than it used to be and we are beginning to see how it can be linked up with normal physics and zoology; although there is a very long way to go as yet.

When several books of mine had been published reporting our investigations in these matters, I received a letter from my publisher asking me whether I would undertake an investigation of dreams in the same sort of manner as that in which we had treated parapsychology. As it happened I did not think that I had many dreams, but I was willing to make the attempt. I was not well read in the subject and could approach it with a completely open mind. It turned out to be most interesting and quite unlike what I had expected. For one thing, I had no idea that I had dreams nearly every night. Over a long period of years I had only remembered about half a dozen. However, once I started to think about it, the things cropped up all the time and I had to write them down. I have about 150 examples of dreams, mostly my own but some from my wife and friends, tabulated and ready for publication if it should prove to be worth while. I shall not quote many here, although a few are necessary.

I can say at once that there seem to be two main types of dream. Apparently one type is a cut from a true dream, brooded over and extended by a sleepy mind. This is probably the kind of thing which interests psychologists. Over it the dreamer's mind seems to hold some kind of control and to a professional it may give some indication of the state of the patient's mentality. The second type appears to be a true dream, beyond the control of the earth mind. It is clear and vivid and may not always belong to the dreamer at all, as at times it seems to be something transmitted by telepathy from somebody else. One at least of mine must have been a hundred years old when I received it. Still, we will not go into this in detail. We have not finished with Dunne.

Dunne was greatly surprised to have a series of dreams which were about matters which had not yet happened and he felt compelled to investigate this theoretically impossible matter. I shall not quote from him. If the reader is keen enough, he will get a copy of *An Experiment with Time* and read the exciting account himself. They are remarkable: volcanic eruptions, terrible fire and other dramatic events, all dreamed of before they took place and mostly derived from newspaper reports as yet unprinted. One indeed contained a numerical error, which was to be in a newspaper when it came out later. In his sleep Dunne was obtaining information about things he was going to read in the papers days later. It was all recorded and timed in a way which could not be shrugged off. Dunne's future memories were as much fact as the landing on the moon.

With his trained observation and keen mind Dunne had discovered something far more important than the flying machines with which he worked, for he had identified another mental level on which things were known before they happened on earth. Compared with this fact, any fault in a mathematical explanation was of little count. He had identified a superconscious level beyond sleep and apparently also beyond death. The theory of the Philosophers that there could be no future life because, after death, there would be no brain and the brain was the fount of all thinking, also became rather shaky. What was the brain doing reading newspapers which had not yet been printed? The idea that mind is distinct from brain and that the brain is no more than a censor for what may be suitable to earth-level thinking appears to answer this particular problem.

Terminology

The Church maintains that a man consists of body, soul and spirit. Here again we have trouble with words. Many times I have tried to get a clear definition of what comprises a soul or a spirit. As far as one can see the terms are synonymous; although I may well be too dense to appreciate the difference. It seems to be easier to regard the thinking part of man as 'mind'. Some people do not like 'mind' and they do not like 'conscience'. The reason for their objection is not clear and probably originates from the idea that there can be no mentality without a brain.

In any case I propose to call whatever part of humanity does the thinking the 'mind'. It may be the same as soul, or it may be spirit. We may not be too far out with the little table shown here.

```
Body   = Body
Soul   = Individual consciousness
Spirit = Mind, possibly much more extensive
Brain  = Censor for earth-level thinking
```

Terminology is made no easier by those who call any form of ghostly phenomenon a spirit. The bulk of such things appear to be no more than natural projections of the same general type as pictures on television, or sounds on radio. They probably differ very little from what we experience in dreams. A visual ghost is a real incident but out of its correct sequence in time. A television picture is exactly the same. Both are products of electronics but the ghost is on a higher frequency and needs no mechanical projector. To call such a phenomenon a spirit is to imply that the observer is looking at a contemporary living entity, which is neither the case with the ghost, nor the television picture. Please notice that I do not say that real entities from another level of existence are never seen. I only state that the bulk of ghostly phenomena are not of this character. On occasion my wife and I have both seen ghosts and spent considerable time and trouble over the problem. Here we might perhaps note that probably about a third of the population is unable ever to see a ghost. Their potential seems to be too low and puts them in a similar category to those who are colour blind or tone deaf. Presumably it is a subconscious sense of their inadequacy that leads a number of people into furious denials of a phenomenon, which is well attested in all countries and in all ages.

Fortunately colour blindness is a recognised handicap and so there are fewer collisions at sea than there might have been, although there are still more than enough. It would be a good thing if psychic blindness, granted that this is a good term for it, could be recognised also; it is easily identified by dowsing. I may have put the numbers of the psychic blind too high. Most modern people are slightly on the positive side, judging from experiments carried out with some 200 people.

Since we have to form our own opinion on these matters, it is a clue which we have to seek and not the pronouncement of some philosopher. Once you have the clue, it is up to you to follow its lead. That is how you extend your mentality and take your part in evolution. What the purpose of this may be, is not our concern; any more than the private soldier can possibly know what is going on in the mind of the Corps or Army Commander. You just see that you are expected to evolve and that is that.

What do we mean by evolve? Once again we have this difficulty with words. Apparently there is evidence for physical evolution, by which one kind of animal is believed to grow into another of higher type. But there is also devolution, through which the legs of a seal, which is believed to have once been a land animal like an otter, have been turned into flippers for convenience in the sea. One seldom hears of devolution. In fact the evolution story as taught to students is a one-sided affair. Everything is called evolution; even if this involved the developing horse in dropping off its toes till it had only one on each foot. Of course this is not evolution at all but devolution. There is no reason to believe me, but I think that our evolution consists of broadening our outlook through contact with a series of sequences of events on the earth level. From each sequence we are expected to draw a conclusion which will help to enlarge our mental range. If you go through a bad patch and, at the end of it, all you can think is how awful it was, you are wasting the opportunity presented by that sequence. There was something in it which could have widened your mental outlook. That is what I mean by a clue. Somewhere in all that trouble and discomfort was something to learn; some point which could not have been brought up except by enduring the sequence.

We do not know why our mental view has to be enlarged; but it seems that this must be something of considerable importance. When looking back over the past sequences of my life, I have observed that whatever one undertook invariably had a relationship to something one was going to do, perhaps many years afterwards. Something in some archaeological investigation would explain what was found in a completely different bit of work decades later. I never did a piece of research work which did not in time fit in with another. For instance a puzzle resulting from an excavation in Cambridgeshire could be solved by something found in a dig in the Hebrides in twenty-five years' time. It needs some practice in observation to notice these points, but they are there if you look for them and must surely imply the existence of some kind of plan for each individual.

Another word, which leads to much confusion, is God. For most of the English-speaking world God is the supreme and unique entity, who created the Universe. But a very high proportion of people either do not believe that God exists, or, if He does, have not the slightest idea what He might be like.

For most of Christendom, since the Dark Ages, God has been thought of and illustrated as an august human father figure with a beard. According to the Bible, God suggested and made man in His own image and so it was reasonable to suppose that God bore some resemblance to the bearded men of the age. But this is mainly based on a Hebrew view of God. Other races had other ideas and some even applied the term to living men with outstanding qualities. Roman Emperors, for instance, became gods and Herod, before his unfortunate infestation with worms, had been hailed as a god. It seems probable that many gods of the ancient world had had their origin in living men who had once been famous in their day. Things become even more confusing when we appreciate that the word 'Devil' in reality refers to a god of a different faith and is not necessarily evil at all. In fact the 'div' or 'dev' part of the word means 'holy'. It is easy to say that this conflict of meanings, when added to that of the difficulty of 'spirit', becomes very complicated for laymen and professional religious alike.

When confronted with a tangle of this sort, and especially a tangle whose origins go back into the mists of time, the best thing to do seems to be to cut out all the dead wood. Then we can regard both God and Spirit as something mental. Let us say that God is Mind. We will no longer regard God as a bearded old man. Man is created with a mind in the image of the Great Creator. The beard is of no importance, for this is not mind but body. In fact man is created with a bit of mind, which can think. There is no reason to suppose that I have got this right, but it may be worth thinking about as we progress in this investigation. Man may be a little bit of mind separated off from the Universal Mind of the Creator of Everything. Of course this does not fit in with the doctrine of chance, but it is really very hard to see how you could get anything at all unless someone started it. Why should there be anything on which chance could operate? Although I cannot bring myself to believe in the old man with a beard, I find the chance idea still less probable. Even man can create to a moderate extent; why should not a much greater mind create far more extensively? To assume, as many do, that any trivial human mind can know the purpose and intention of a mind which can sprinkle the Universe with numberless stars, seems to me to be little more than gross presumption. To get any sense out of the idea, it seems necessary to assume the existence of a vast hierarchy of minds in descending order from the Great One at the top to the tiny human specimen beneath. But it might go much farther than this, with a spark of mind existing in every living organism.

I hope to show presently that man appears to have the ability of detaching portions of his mind and locating these in the things he makes or uses. In this way perhaps our assumed hierarchy could be formed. It would be thought into existence and each unit would be an image of the Creator; not in bodily appearance, but in the way in which it thought. It is interesting to note that this story of the creation of man in God's image is not confined to the Bible but is found in much the same form in the pre-Spanish legends of America.

The study of thought is of fundamental importance. With it you seem to be able to create. It is the force with which Mind operates. Enlarge your thinking and you extend your mind. Do not do so, or rely on the products of other people's thinking, and you are more useless than a slug creeping on the surface of the earth.

For evolution appears to be a command from the Creator of the Universe, though it differs very much from the evolution of the Darwin and Huxley variety. Although I have taken little interest in the theory of reincarnation, yet it seems very probable that those who cannot be bothered to develop their minds will have to return to earth again after death and do the whole business again.

It may be of interest to describe one of my attempts to investigate the old gods. There was a god of the sea, Manannan, to whom the Celts of Britain paid homage. Very little is recorded about him, yet his name remains in Clackmannan in Scotland, which means Manannan's stone. There are also well-known hobby-horse rituals performed on May Day down the coast of Devon and Cornwall by sea fishermen and it is assumed that the hobby-horses may well be the white horses of the sea, who also belonged to Poseidon. Therefore one might suspect that Poseidon and Manannan are two names for the one god. This happens to most ancient gods. Isis was said to have a thousand names.

Yet who really thinks that there was such an entity as Poseidon? I can't say that it seems possible today to visualise anyone of the sort. But, if for hundreds of years men concentrated their thoughts on a figure of this kind and wished fervently for its help, what would happen? Each one probably detached something of his mind into the creation of this non-existent figure. Poseidon became a mass of detached thoughts and there was a Poseidon. I think he would not be what we call alive in an earthly sense. But he would be a cloud of force, which some might be able to tap. We surely must not look on the old gods as never having existed. They existed as long as men believed in their existence. The old witches still believe that they can see them if they go through the correct ritual.

It is well recorded that the fishermen of the North of Lewis used to wade into the sea at the beginning of the fishing season and pour a libation of beer to a sea god, who has been named as Shoney. I do not think that this was his name but simply a distortion of the Gaelic for Holy One.

Recently I read a book by Lilian Beckwith called *Green Hand*. This interested me for it was a careful study of the fishing life of Mallaig and the Western Islands. Miss Beckwith included a curious jingle. I felt she must have heard it aboard a fishing boat at a party described in the book. The little rhyme went like this:

Ickle, Ockle, Blue Bockle,
    Fishes in the Sea.
If you're looking for a lover,
    Please choose me.

It was the 'Blue Bockle', which caught my eye. For Bocan is a godling in Gaelic and Bogle is the same in Scots. Blue Bockle is a blue godling and presumably he came from the Outer Hebrides. Then I got down to the whole rhyme. It is a quaint mixture of Scots and Gaelic. I think it can be translated like this:

Little, youthful, blue godling
(Of the) fishes of the sea.
If you're looking for devotion,
Please choose me.

This appears to be the charm, which the men of Lewis called to Shoney when they poured beer into the sea. For many years I had waited for this clue. The Blue Men of the Minch were gods.

Now the normal Celtic god has three phases (or personalities), young, prime of life, and old. There would be three Blue Men, or just possibly nine, for each phase in turn might be triple. The Blue Bockle was the young one. To the old one (probably called bodach gorm) they sacrificed cattle. Are our coastwise hobby-horses with their emphasis on fertility, the steeds of the god in his prime? I think it is very likely, and we have the whole cycle of the worship of Manannan. I don't know if Poseidon was blue, but I seem to remember that he was dark. Even when ashore he was associated with white horses and fertility; while black bulls were thrown into the sea in his honour. It looks very much as if Poseidon and Manannan are synonymous.

How would you describe a god of this kind? I think it would be as a cloud of past memories; but it is to some extent animated by the combined minds of those who created it. It can probably be seen and most certainly it can be felt.

A single individual can produce a ghost or ghoul by his thought or memory projected into an electromagnetic field. Many people together in a similar way can project a mass thought or memory and it becomes known as a god or a demon. Both types really belong to the second mental level on which time does not appear to operate and so to earth-living minds they may appear in past or future time. Without some other interference they would never end at all. The gods are immortal.

3 Dreams

Although many people may deny the possibility of seeing ghosts, it is quite absurd to say that no one experiences dreams. It is now supposedly possible to tell with instruments if a sleeping person is dreaming. Dreams are respectable: ghosts are not. Yet there seems to be much in common between the two phenomena. They both belong to a different level of awareness from the one normally used in waking life. However, scientists will accept somebody's story of what he dreamt and be blankly incredulous if the same person describes a ghost which he has appreciated. It is a curious blind spot in the scientist's own make-up and the reverse of the true scientific outlook. A witness should be believed until he can be shown to be wrong. If a scientist can pick and choose what observations he will accept, it makes others wonder how much reliance they can put on his reports of his personal findings. What has he left out because it did not fit in with some preconceived theory? One knows of several cases where this has been done and which thereby created a completely false picture. Fortunately we are now about to deal with dreams and so there is a reasonable chance that what we report may be believed.

As I said before, there are two main classes of what may be called dreams. Over one our waking mind seems to have some measure of control and, by its imagination, it can mould the progress of the dream. The second class is a true dream and appears to be completely uninfluenced by the waking mind. It is an experience on another level of consciousness and from these experiences we can derive a great deal of unexpected information. Here is one, which at once attracted my attention.

On 23 October 1970, I had a clear dream in colour (as most of mine are). I appeared to see, for in reality it was pitch dark, something like a brown, furry snake coming into the room beside my bed. The snake was followed by a brown lump attached to it and perhaps nine inches above the floor. Very soon a complete brownish cat had come into the room backwards. I memorised the furniture and when properly

Figure 1 The dream of the reversing cat. From memory: A. The tail appears. B. The whole cat comes into view.

awake drew a picture of the whole incident (Figure 1). Of course cats do walk backwards along window ledges and things of that sort, but it is not their normal method of locomotion. The more I thought of it, the more probable it seemed that the dream cat was not really coming backwards into the room, but was going out of it. When I reversed the drawing of the furniture in the looking-glass, it was clear that I was looking at a slightly distorted picture of our own bedroom as seen from my bed (Figure 2). The cat was our Siamese, Hecate. Others have experienced reversed dreams of this nature and this reversal is evidently reasonably common. But it raises problems. How

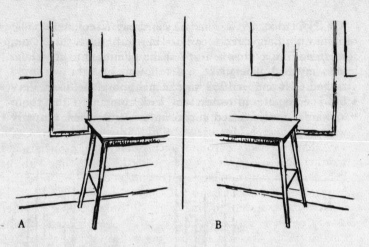

Figure 2 Two sketches to demonstrate the apparent reversal of a locality as seen in dream. A. Part of our bedroom as seen from my bed. B. The same view when reversed. Compare memory of dream (Figure 1).

does one's mind run backwards? Every natural phenomenon must have a natural explanation and the reversed picture of Hecate became in the end a most important clue.

The recording of dreams does make us take trouble, for what one appears to be observing passes very quickly, like a picture on a cinema or television screen. It is shot apparently on one mental level and appreciated, like a memory, on the next. The observer has to cultivate the art of catching it, like the good portrait painter catches the fleeting expression of his sitter, and this may be a very difficult art to master.

Apparently the dream is a sequence on a different level of mentality from that used in earth life and it probably passes much more swiftly likewise. If you study a lot of dreams it appears that the same sequence takes place on each level. One is a replica of the other, even if there are some differences in observation. We see here that we are getting very close to Dunne's series of observers; but there is a difference. In dreams each observer does not see exactly the same picture as the first one does.

I regret that my dreams are short and uninteresting. There are no thrilling events comparable to those which Dunne recorded; but perhaps their very simplicity makes it easier to see what is happening.

On 24 November 1969, I woke in the middle of the night. As I did so I appeared to see the face of a man I did not know, looking at me. I seemed to see him through a looking-glass as it were. Although his features were quite distinct and one could see that he had a round face somewhat bronzed and weather-beaten, it was not clear what he was doing with his hands, which were moving about round his chin. I assumed that he was soaping his face before shaving.

Next day we were driving from Sidford to Sidbury, rather slowly on that winding road. On one bend I looked straight into the front of a car approaching us from Sidbury. At the wheel was the man whom I had seen in my dream. He was leaning back and his hands were sawing at the wheel on the level of his chin. I had mistaken the frame of the windscreen for a looking-glass.

I could report many dreams of this kind, for I have them all written down and dated. Some are things I was going to see in newspapers in a few days' time; some are shots from future television and so on. Generally there is some slight difference between the two experiences, but the identity is clear. Dream memories can be and frequently are in future time. I am afraid this is a fact which we are saddled with and, upsetting though it may be, it needs a rational answer. I do not know whether everybody has future dreams, but all the people I have asked to note their experiences have had some in future time. It is certainly more common than the reversed type.

We have been confronted with two types of situation, which to our grandparents would have appeared utterly impossible. How could an event happen backwards, or how could the future exist? But these things are fact, not imagination nor delusion. One suspects at once that, in some way which we cannot for the moment see, the dilemma's horn of time is poking into the picture. One remembers the extract from a pilot's log during the 1914 war: 'Passed a seagull flying backwards!' Something must have made our cat appear to walk backwards, because the observer is in some way moving faster than the cat appears to be doing. But the observer is apparently asleep, or nearly so, in bed. It appears that the observer on the next mental level must be going faster.

At present we know nothing about this observer at all, except that he seems to be so tightly linked to our earth personality that he apparently experiences the same sequences of events. Which comes first, the egg or the chicken? Or are both sequences identical? They cannot be identical or the cat would not progress backwards. But they might be like identical strips of film exposures starting at the same moment and run through at different speeds.

If this were so, it would account both for the cat (like the seagull in the report) and for occurrences in future time. It would depend on the speeds of the two projections. This is rather difficult to visualise but I think most people today will understand what I mean. From this we can surely infer that during sleep our minds are still operating, but at a different speed from what they do when we are awake on earth. The body may be at rest but the mind is still busy. One imagines that it is playing through the strip of film, which the earth consciousness was experiencing while it was awake. One might think it was checking the thing through in the same sort of way as that in which an author corrects his proofs. This seems to me to diminish greatly the importance of the brain, for this is not apparently being used. The whole operation is in the mind and there is no evidence that the second observer has any connection with the brain at all. He may have very little connection with the observer on earth, except to use the film, which that observer has made for him. Or that observer may be a projection of himself and sent out to gather information. I incline towards the second view, but let us see what happens as we go on with the investigation.

I have a pen friend, Mrs V. Beresford, who lives in the Beaconsfield area. I have never met her. She is a very keen and efficient research worker in all these odd subjects. On 30 November 1969, I woke to see a small, highly-coloured bird of the parrot family peering out of some box or hole. I did not take much notice of the bird, for a strange voice was speaking. I could hear the words, which seemed to be: 'Budgie is very peeved. His sole of rubber . . . has been spotted.' That morning I wrote to Mrs Beresford and told her about this dream. By return of post, sent on 2 December, I had a letter from her saying she had received mine and had been very surprised by what it said, for on 1 December a strange budgerigar had flown in through her window. She had put it in a spare cage and remarked to a neighbour: 'A budgie, he's pleased. He knew somehow he'd have a safe harbour here.'

This was even more remarkable than the other two dreams. First I had experienced a dream memory in future time. I got this memory at a different time of day from that at which the incident really happened. Therefore it could not have been a case of ordinary telepathy, or thought transference. Then, although the words I apparently heard were not the same as those which were spoken a hundred miles away in Beaconsfield, their sound, probably not remembered exactly by either of us, was so similar that one can hardly doubt that they were the same. Since my earth observer was asleep, the whole incident appears to argue some kind of telepathic communication between Mrs Beresford's observer two and my observer two. Further than this, the whole thing suggests a very great deal of activity on the part of the observers on the second level. The incident was so trivial that clearly much else must pass between the two observers. One might think that they study each other's films. I am inclined to think that those who believe that they are to enjoy a period of laziness and rest when they die are in for a considerable surprise.

Mind is perhaps eternal and the part of it you use in daily life just a very small fraction of the whole. Of course I am guessing now, but as we go on we may come upon more clues, which may help to make the guesses more informed. Guesses, even if they are wrong, are useful, for they stir up people to think out what is wrong with them. It is the lack in original thought which has left us with this dilemma for so long. People are afraid to think and even more afraid to try out their ideas on others.

Water Divining, Dowsing and Pendulum

Now that we have sketched out roughly some observations about dreams, it becomes necessary to use an entirely different approach to get at a better understanding.

Water divining has been known for so long that there is no possibility of ever locating the place where it was first used. In all likelihood it was much employed by primitive man and many a moss-grown spring (known as a well in the Highlands) surrounded by a ring of stones was first discovered with a hazel twig. There were few communities in Britain without someone who could divine water. It was a faculty known to all and accepted as a natural gift. Although other human faculties were so obvious that they had to be accepted, the men who elevated themselves to be rulers of thought in the realm of science would not believe in its existence.

It was a curious flaw in a world which was very efficient and hard-working in most ways, and a strange block limiting many roads of expanding vision. In an extremely simple way it has at last been appreciated that the faculty exists. Once it has been accepted, cloaked in a mass of technical jargon, it will extend considerably. Fred and his fork of hazel will become a thing of the past. At least I fear that this will happen; because Fred will be so awed by all the clever talk, that, instead of finding a blocked drain for himself, he will call in somebody from the appropriate ministry, complete with an instrument costing hundreds of pounds and will have to wait months before this wonder appears.

The subject is so vast that it would provide hundreds of research workers with a life work for many generations. Water divining is only a tiny facet of the whole thing, for this concerns the complete science of a higher level of human mentality. It is only through a partial study of divination that we have begun to understand thi..

Although I have known for many years that I could find hidden water movements and have even found a lost Anglo-Saxon cemetery by the same method, I took no great interest in the possibilities until we had left Cambridge and returned to live in our native West Country. Early in our life back here there was a long summer drought and not enough water to drive the hydraulic ram. We had an alternative water supply but it was clear that the ram ought to be started again by clearing the spring outlets leading to it. There was no plan of where these outlets were and a five-acres field to search. I remembered my experiments in divination years before and cut some hazel forks from the wood. There was no difficulty at all. I found four sources of water, within less than a yard of their positions, in an afternoon. Nothing showed on the surface of the field, although the pipes from two springs ran through a dry, mediaeval fish pond. This was quite enough to convince anyone with normal intelligence that water divining was a useful fact and not useless nonsense.

The hazel fork is hardly an instrument of precision. You cannot observe within a hand's breadth where the movement takes place. Wishing for a more exact instrument, I turned to something I had read long before. This was a pamphlet by a French brigadier, who in the First World war had located German mines in the sea with a pendulum. The soldier has to train his powers of observation, and he travels about the world. Therefore he has a chance to learn something. I doubt if you could find any regiment without one or two acute observers in its ranks. So when a brigadier said he could locate mines with a pendulum, I believed him and made one for myself.

This was the beginning of an adventure, which changed so many of my old ways of thinking that I can hardly remember what they were like before. I know now that there is a part of our mental make-up whose knowledge infinitely exceeds anything we meet in life on earth and that there is a way of talking to this mental part in a kind of code. The finding of hidden water with a divining rod is just a small part of the whole thing. Our code can tell us where a minute pin is buried under undisturbed turf, or whether someone you are tracing has an illness on the other side of the world.

Years ago children used to know how to handle this code with a pendulum and find hidden objects with it by the roadside. I do not know if the scientists were aware that the pendulum was an alternative to, and more exact instrument than, the divining rod. If they did, the same mental block prevented them from investigating it also. I have known many great scientists, just as I have known field-marshals, and I do not blame them at all. It is the nineteenth-century pundits, who chained them into one particular method, who are to blame.

I have frequently described the operation of the pendulum in such books as *Ghost and Divining Rod*, but I must repeat some of the details here for what it appears to tell us is vital to our inquiry. The answers may be similar to those given by people known as sensitives, or mediums, but the method of obtaining them is quite distinct. It should be remembered that a good water diviner does not need a rod at all and can divine simply by the feelings in his fingers. The child with a cotton reel on a string looking for pennies beside a road uses the same power in a very elementary way as the full-fledged medium, who goes into a trance and apparently into another level altogether. For you have to have a mind operating in conjunction with the pendulum or divining rod, or whatever instrument is being used. None of it is purely mechanical and though electric gadgets are being produced for this purpose at considerable expense, you still need a human operator to work them. This is the great point. There is no magic virtue in the gadget itself and it is no more than a code for conversation between two levels of mind.

Fortunately I took up this study before it became respectable in England (it has of course been popular for many years in France) and so I did not find it much encumbered with technical terms. Now that the existence of water divining has been recognised at Cambridge, it will not be long before they start to come off the conveyor belt in hundreds, adding greatly to the difficulties of understanding. For the moment we can be satisfied with very few. First there is the pendulum itself. It does not seem to matter what it is made of, from chewing gum to ivory. I use a simple ball of hazel wood about an inch in diameter. A couple of yards of thread are pegged with a matchstick into a hole in this ball (or bob as some call it). The other end of the thread is wound round a short rod (or windlass) of about the thickness of a pencil, so that the ball can be raised or lowered by revolving the rod, like a miniature windlass, between the forefinger and thumb. A steel tape is useful for measuring the length of thread unwound. That is positively all the apparatus needed, or ever will be for that matter; although we may be sure that most elaborate things will be designed to take its place. I am a little doubtful about nylon thread, for nylon is said to interrupt various rays. I use ordinary linen thread.

The length of thread from the top of the bob of the pendulum to the bottom point from which it is suspended is known as the 'rate'. This is an older technical term and can be used here without causing confusion. Practically speaking it is the only term I find necessary to use.

I have dwelt on this because I hope to encourage others to make investigations for themselves and find (as many write to say they do) that they get the same results as I have done. There is simplicity about the whole thing, which is quite surprising. One thinks of Newton's apple and Stephenson's kettle. Simplicity seems to be a pointer to the right road.

Although the general idea may be simple, this is no indication that the continuation will not be most complicated. This is certainly the case with divination.

Having obtained a pendulum, you find very quickly and easily how it reacts. The simplest of all its foibles is the well-known one of sexing unborn children by suspending a wedding ring on a piece of thread above the mother-to-be's middle. For male it will move one way (backwards and forwards I fancy); for female another (probably a circular swing). This has been known and practised for untold ages and has been elaborated by many dowsers; but the old French brigadier had a way which seems far more exact.

The simple short method in general use needs seven inches of thread or less. In practice it only seems capable of saying yes or no. It will tell you if food is going to suit you, if you swing the pendulum very gently between you and the dish. If the swing becomes circular, it is advisable not to eat it. Frenchmen often use this. But to get wider information dowsers have to make use of samples of what they wish to find and they call these witnesses. With the brigadier's long pendulum only a steel tape is needed. You can carry most numbers you are likely to need in your head, or use a small notebook of tables.

The method is this: every thought, whether concrete or abstract, appears to have a series of co-ordinates, which enables one's superconscious to isolate it instantly. They seem to be like a much more extensive telephone directory and we have only found the first pages of it.

I will try to explain how it works. Take some object (I usually suggest a silver teaspoon) and put it on the floor. Hold the windlass of the pendulum above it between your thumb and forefinger and unroll it very slowly. Keep the bob swinging very slightly backwards and forwards (that is oscillating). At a certain length a hesitation comes over the oscillation and after about another half inch the pendulum movement turns into a circular swing (a gyration). This is the 'rate' for silver. In practice it is 22 inches. Experiment also shows that other things have this same rate. Lead, calcium and sodium have it and so does the colour grey. So the rate on the pendulum is not enough to distinguish silver. I had a lot of trouble in finding this out and was frequently confused when looking for silver by finding pieces of salt-glazed pottery, which were covered with calcium carbonate. The pieces of salt-glazed pottery reacted to several minerals: calcium 22 inches, carbon 12, oxygen 27, silica 14, and so on.

After a lot of experiment, it was found that the 'rate' was qualified by a second factor. When tuned in to a given object, the pendulum made a number of gyrations and then returned to a back and forth swing. Silver reacted to a rate of 22 inches and made 22 circular swings, but the colour grey only made 7 gyrations while calcium made 30. It was clear that for our pendulum code, you could write down 22:22 for silver and 22:7 for grey. For oxidised silver both would be correct. This code is much more detailed than that you can find with a short pendulum and witnesses. You can examine the surface of a piece of turf, using your forefinger as a radar scanner, and note where there are reactions. If the reaction is 22:30 it should be a scrap of salt glaze, or perhaps a snail shell (largely composed of calcium carbonate). When you have found the rates for a large number of minerals and the number of turns which they make, you can explore an undisturbed piece of ground and have a very good idea what is concealed beneath its grassy surface. You yourself, with your five senses, could not possibly know this. The pendulum would appear to be putting you in touch with something which does know. One does not believe this at first; you have to work hard at experiment. Once you are convinced that these rods and pendulums do work, then a view of life begins to form which is quite new.

One of the most remarkable facts to emerge from experiment is that the pendulum deals with abstract ideas as well as concrete ones. For instance, love is provided with co-ordinates 20:20, in the same way as iron or copper. In fact the pendulum is dealing with thought forms and not with the kinds of thing you can measure in a laboratory. It is the idea in one's mind of a pin beneath the ground which it will demonstrate for you and not the solid metal object as we believe it to be in ordinary life. You can dig up the pin and it will be hidden exactly where the pendulum said it was, but it was the mental impression which was shown to you in code.

The consideration of the phenomena becomes more difficult when it is realised that everything the pendulum can find (that is, every thought form) has an electromagnetic field of its own, or something like it, and we can study the shape of this field. The pendulum seems to be detecting what might perhaps be described as 'rays of thought'. What you send out like a radar beam must be a ray of your own thought. When the pendulum gyrates, it is because this ray has met the obstruction (i.e. the object of your thought) and has been turned back on itself. The bob can no longer swing back and forth and has to revert to a circular motion. We are dealing with the mechanics of some form of psychology and learning something about thought in a most unorthodox manner. The bob on a bit of thread seems to be introducing us to a superconscious mind. Whether this is our own mind, or something with a wider province of perhaps several minds, remains to be seen. Whatever it is, its knowledge, or power of obtaining knowledge, is vast. You send it a brief message: 'I would like some copper', and it promptly shows you in exact detail where to dig up a pin and how deep that pin is in the ground. It is even more remarkable when it can tell all kinds of details about some unknown person who has written you a letter. Of course this was magic, but it is now science. It became a science directly Cambridge admitted that water divining really took place.

We surely have something here, which has a bearing on our dilemma. The subconscious has been talked about for a long time and does not seem a particularly attractive part of our make-up. One suspects that some of its attributes are not subconscious at all but in reality form small factors in the superconscious, which has hardly come into the picture today. If I have added it up correctly, man seems to consist of three consciousnesses (sub, earth and super). He also appears to be an animal provided with a superior mind. It seems reasonable to assume that the subconscious represents the animal portion of the composition and that the superconscious is what he is intended to develop into. This is guessing again; but it is difficult to see how any form of chance evolution could possibly have produced this composite figure. The whole thing looks much more like a deliberate experiment conducted by some entity on an infinitely higher level than anything we could possibly know about.

We have no idea why this should be done; but then we have no conception why the midnight sky should be spangled with stars. It is surely only conceit which makes men think that they understand it all. If they were living on the superconscious level they might possibly know a little more about it and, if they had a code through which they could talk to the superconscious, there might be a chance of learning something. It is clear that there is some kind of block between each level of consciousness. A pendulum or some other gadget is needed before you can make contact with your superconscious, unless you are a medium and then as a rule it is only possible if you are in a trance; although many people have flashes of mediumistic 'sight' without any gadget being necessary. During sleep the mind appears to be operating on a higher level and the block is then the opposite way round. It is not easy to convey to the earth mind what the superconscious has been doing during this sleep, but there is an attempt to tell the story in many dreams.

Out of the Body Experiences

There are people who can control their visits into the higher
mental level and report back to some extent what they have
experienced; we have known one of these. Although it is hard
to believe the reports, they appear to be genuine. Once again
there was a clue and, although I have published it before, I must
tell it again. Very briefly then what happened was this.

Some time ago a lady lived near us, who had studied magic
and claimed to be an adept. She often came and talked to me.
She taught me how to prevent the arrival of unwanted visitors
by putting pentagrams in their way. Before going to sleep one
night, I practised drawing mental pentagrams round our beds. I
was not greatly interested in this kind of magic and was simply
amused to see if I could draw mental pentagrams.

A few nights later my wife woke feeling that somebody was
in the room and saw a faint light moving round the beds before
it faded out.

About a fortnight later our magician friend dropped in for
tea. She wanted to know if someone had been putting
protection on us. I replied that they hadn't as far as I knew but
why did she ask. She said that she came into our bedroom one
night to see if we were all right but she could not get near the
bed because of the triangles of fire round it. It turned out that
she was in the habit of visiting her friends' houses by going on
to another mental level and travelling on it. This is not
evidence, but the pentagram business is very remarkable.
Strange though it seemed to us, it was evidently commonplace
to an adept. She claimed to fly quite easily from place to place
and much enjoyed the sensation.

There are many accounts of people doing this kind of thing
and describing what they have seen during their travels. They
claim to be still joined to their sleeping bodies by an extensible
silver cord, which is mentioned in the Bible, and some
deliberately train themselves to do this. There are even greater
numbers who get involved by chance. During illness, or under
anaesthetics, or as a result of an accident, they suddenly find
themselves out of their earth bodies.

I have not experienced this but I have had letters from and

talked to others who have had it. One was a Church of England parson who, when taking a service, suddenly found himself outside and above his body and could watch what it was doing. There are examples of the same type reported in Dr Raynor Johnson's books. Here is one sent to me by a correspondent:

> You mention that you have met people, who when near death, have sometimes seen their physical bodies from the outside. I once experienced this at the dentist's after having gas. I seemed to be floating in a corner near the ceiling, slightly to the left of the chair where my 'body' sat. I could see the back of my head, and the dentist bending over as if he was searching my face for a sign of consciousness. Then a strong magnetic current drew me back to the body. I fitted into it with perfect smoothness, and found myself looking with my physical eyes into the dentist's eyes. He uttered the vulgar word: 'SPIT.'

This is very clearly described and can be taken as a typical case. The experience can be brought on by fever, hypnosis and accident, as well as in a dream; while some people claim to be able to achieve this condition at will. It is evident that the person concerned moves temporarily on to the second whorl of the spiral, where in my theory he should be above and to the left of his physical body. The condition appears to be a limited form of death.

The point, which strikes me as important, as I hope to discuss later, is that the person on his second level of consciousness finds himself to one side and above his body. The displacement frequently seems to be of the same degree. He is about 6½ feet above and perhaps 2 feet to one side of his body. I think that this is very important. Assuming that in a sequence of events experienced by the body the mind is located where that body is, on a second mental level the mind is located about 80 inches farther from the centre of the earth. This ought to give us the clue to the difference in the rates of vibration between the two mental levels. I will try later to express this in the form of a diagram based on what the pendulum has to tell us. For the moment it is enough to guess that life on the second level is four times as fast as that on earth. Yet, unlike the earth, it apparently has no moving time. Presumably the first-level mind sets the sequence in motion; although this again is a guess.

One thing is clear: if my reasoning from what is observed fact is correct, then no person with a normal rate of vibration on earth would in ordinary circumstances be able to see people or events on higher levels. They would take place well outside the earth spectrum. Here is one facet of the block between the levels of existence. Those with mediumistic powers, who do get through the block, must somehow have their normal rate of vibration speeded up considerably. Thus our magician friend was only visible in our bedroom as a small light. This is frequently reported by Hindu and other advanced thinkers in India, who are said to leave their bodies and move across country as balls of light. It is possible that the phenomenon of foo-fighters, frequently noted during the Second World War by observers in aeroplanes and inexplicable to ordinary science, indicates that dead airmen from the next levels still took an interest in what was going on and followed the planes with their superconscious minds. We may imagine perhaps that they had not yet realised which mental level they were on.

Therefore it is quite impossible for anyone to state with truth that he knows there is no continuation of earth life on another level. He cannot know this; although he might find the opposite true, if he knew how to speed up his vibrations.

If then we have a code by which we can correspond with the superconscious however weakly, it should be possible to find out, or at least infer, the answer to this and many other questions. These answers will have none of the glamour of those obtained from a medium, but will bear some similarity to those produced by a computer. In each case the question has to be fed from a human mind into an inanimate mechanism, which yields the result. Neither computer nor pendulum can produce results on its own. There must be mental direction of the apparatus. The weakness of both lies in the intelligence of the operator. Many ships are doomed to strand on this reef. How are you to be sure of the intelligence of the man who proposes the questions?

4   Debates on Dreams

In the appendix, we have brought together quite a lot of
information derived from human guinea pigs, who were not
neurotics and were as well-balanced as we could find. This was
with the object of starting from the normal and from there
trying to build up a framework on which later information on
dreams could be hung. It was not thought for a moment that
any complete picture was likely to emerge; but it was hoped
that some general ideas might be forthcoming. We have not
been disappointed. Quite a number of interesting facts have
come to light and now we will try to evaluate them against
other facets of what is sometimes called 'The Odd'.

I suppose The Odd has been properly defined somewhere;
but I do not happen to have seen it. It has many branches and
all of them present features which do not fit in with normal
physical science. Some (like hypnosis) have become respectable. Telepathy is widely accepted. Yet others, although
vouched for by innumerable observers, are still regarded with
suspicion and disdain. Nobody in his senses disbelieves that
mankind has dreams; but ghosts, which seem to be much the
same kind of phenomenon, are flatly denied by half the
educated world. Until quite recently very many scientists
refused to believe that water and oil can be found by a diviner;
although firms run by hard-headed business men often
employed one and such logical (so we are told) people as the
French and Dutch police often used them in their hunt for
criminals. All this incredulity is a hangover from Victorian
science, which could only believe in things which it could weigh
and measure. The Odd cannot be measured and so it cannot

exist of course. Since it obviously does exist, more and more scientists are coming to the somewhat shamefaced acceptance of it. Psychology, although I must say that much of it appears to rest on very shaky foundations, has now a place in respectable studies and to it belongs the study of dreams.

My wife and I became involved in the examination of The Odd through the curiosity which was aroused by actually coming in contact with it. When you experience these things yourself, it is no longer possible to sit back and say: 'Science, or the Pope, or someone or other, says that they cannot exist, therefore they do not exist.' At least you cannot do this without deluding yourself. We saw ghosts and therefore knew that there were such things, whatever the explanation might be. We could find water with a twig and dig it up exactly where the twig told us that it ran. And that is as far as many people ever get.

However, we were eaten up with curiosity and it became an absolute necessity to find out, if it were in any way possible, how these things worked and what caused them. There is no end to the study. When you think you have come to a place where you can leave it and do a little mild gardening, up crops another puzzle and off you go again.

It soon became clear, after what had been observed about the manner in which ghosts were seen, that there was a family likeness between them and the persons seen in dreams. The ghosts do not often appear to be living entities, but something projected by human minds. It is just the same with dreams. Although you see and appear to talk with real living people, many of these seem to be similar to photographic projections. They are only real as far as a projection from a lantern slide is real.

Of course we all know there is considerable doubt among philosophers as to whether anything is real at all. However, this is simply begging the question. As living persons some things are real to us and some are not. A projection from beyond our level of realness is not real to us and, as far as practical purposes go, these dreams and ghosts are not real, at any rate when you are living on the earth plane.

Of course that does not discount the possibility that they

may be as real to people living on another level as our
neighbours here are to us; although I do not think that many of
our ghosts and dream figures are of this nature. The entities
seen by clairvoyants seem to be living persons and not
projections by living persons. There is an important distinction
here, which is often overlooked by people who write to me
complaining that I say there is no such thing as the supernatural
when they have had personal experience of it. Supernatural is a
misnomer. Nothing can be supernatural except whatever
brought the whole of nature into being. Nature is not confined
to one small planet but extends beyond the one galaxy (in
which that planet is found) to cover the whole of creation. It
also exists in layers of vibrational depth to cover whatever
happens to entities on planes higher than our own. Ghosts are
as natural as a foxglove or thrush and so are the projections
which you meet in dreams. But that does not make them real in
the sense that a fox terrier is real. Their degree of reality is the
same as the picture you watch on the TV screen, neither more
nor less.

After spending some months in trying to collect and study
dreams, various points became clearer. The first is that the
distinction between true dreams and what we might call
drowsy thinking, is not at all sharp. Much of what we usually
regard as dreaming is just a slipshod form of re-thinking recent
events and problems. We turn over memories and we fuss over
half-realised difficulties. This kind of thinking is not true
dreaming at all, but it can become mixed with it and you can
spend a lot of drowsy thought in turning over a real dream. The
true dream can come through the other condition like a sudden
beam of bright light. You can also experience one dream
cutting clean through another. I think it is reasonable to regard
the two states as being subconscious and superconscious. The
subconscious is lower than true waking thought and the
superconscious is something at a higher level, which we pass
through when going still higher in sleep. The astonishing thing
about the superconscious is that it appears to know about
many matters which have not yet happened at all. If one
experiments in detail with dowsing, it is easily shown that the
breadth of knowledge of the superconscious is infinitely

greater than that of the ordinary conscious mind on earth. It can find out what is going wrong with other people's bodies on the other side of the world. It can find out swiftly and with very little trouble where things are concealed, utterly beyond the range of human senses. In fact its range is so great that the ordinary earth mind appears trivial by comparison with it. Yet there seems no reason for thinking that it is not our own mind on another level of vibration. It seems to be what we are going to become when we have finished our lives on earth and what we are when we are in deep sleep. This may be a very daring thing to say; but it is the reasoned conclusion to which all the evidence which we have collected seems to point.

This is the place where it is necessary to try to classify the dreams we have collected. A classification can always be changed, yet it is useful to have one. For then you can say to yourself, 'This is a flash type', or 'a Dunne type' and disregard the others while you are examining it.

(1) The first in importance I call the Dunne type. Dunne was the discoverer of the remarkable fact that many dreams of many people contain elements that can be shown to take place after the dream happens. From any point of view this is a momentous discovery. Many people have proved to themselves that it takes place and nobody has explained how it can possibly be so. Therefore the Dunne type contains something in future time.

(2) The second type I regard as the 'flash'. It is a picture, often of an unknown person, which appears on the screen of the mind instantaneously. It is quite distinct from anything which may have been going on before it appeared. There seems to be little difference between this type of dream and the waking appreciation of a lantern slide projection, or a single television 'shot'. Sometimes these pictures do not come on correctly and give all the appearance of a lantern projector being handled carelessly. Some shots seem to have been based on photographs; others on postcards, or magazine illustrations. In no case do they appear to be actual memories of living persons. The flash type may be combined with the Dunne type in that its origin may be recognised after the dream has taken place.

An extension of the flash dream is one which might be called the strip type. It is apparently a flash dream in motion, and closely resembles a length of cinema, or television, film. It comes on instantly and is cut off in the same way. While the suggestion may appear to be absurd, it seems hard to doubt that these lengths of film are projected in some unknown way. This is especially noticeable in the cases of Mrs Beresford and my dreams, which have come on back to front. For convenience these could be styled 'reversed' dreams, but they are only a variant of the strip or flash types. There is a strong suggestion that these reversed specimens could be due to the carelessness of some operator, possibly oneself.

(3) Another kind, which is often linked to the 'strip', is a short scrap of conversation. Conversational dreams seem to have nothing to do with the dreamer and appear to be accidental. A single phrase, or a couple of sentences, may be all that is noted. They are like scraps of talk overheard when passing through a room where someone is telephoning. The dreamer is not doing the talking. Apparently it is being done by strangers. Much importance too must lie in the fact that, like an overheard telephone talk, only one side of the conversation is audible.

There are quite a large number of dreams which show clearly that they are derived, in some unknown way, from somebody other than the dreamer. In one case a dreamer had a dream several times about doings at a house which he had never visited. In another the incidents which appeared in the dream must have taken place at least a hundred years earlier than the dream. I call these dreams 'induced telepathic'. They seem to leak in some unknown way from one human field of force to another. The process seems to ignore ordinary earth ideas of time and of distance also. (Mrs Beresford at Beaconsfield is over a hundred miles from Branscombe.)

(4) Readers will have noticed that I have said nothing about erotic dreams, which seem so important to most students of the subject. The reason is that I think their importance has been considerably exaggerated. I suppose everybody has had an occasional erotic dream, but like 'shock' dreams I think they are probably caused by pressures in the body on certain nerves. The effects of these pressures are half realised and brooded over by a partially awakened mind. Imagination is called into play

and an erotic situation is conjured up, which is really not a dream at all.

(5) Shock dreams take the form of violent jumps in the sleeping body. I have, when awake, often asked my wife why she has jumped convulsively in bed. She has answered in her sleep: 'Someone threw a ball at me.' It was evident that the cause was internal pressure acting on some nerve and causing imagination to react.

It is clear that permutations and combinations may occur of several types of dream at one time and the mixture may be contemplated by the mind itself in a drowsy state and this may add imagination to the resulting muddle. It is also clear that short examples of true dreams, lacking any admixture of waking elements, frequently occur and it is from the examination of these that we may hope to learn something of interest.

It is my object now to try to tackle the various types, which we have extracted, and see whether we can make any sense of them. I must say once more that it is really up to the individual to make this study for himself. What he reads here is second-hand and he has no means of judging whether I have observed correctly or recorded exactly. He does not need a vast compendium of psychological terms; in fact these are a hindrance. All he has to do is to observe, note and think.

To the ordinary person time is something which ticks away at an even rate from birth to death. What then can it possibly mean when many people have dreams of an event before that event takes place? It is an apparent impossibility and yet it happens. What is even more extraordinary is the fact that Dunne and others clearly obtained their dream information from newspapers which had not yet been printed.

There have always been a few people scattered through the mass of the population who knew about events before they actually happened. How a scientist could deny this and yet remain a Christian is hard to see, for the Gospels report Jesus Himself as making prophecies. What is more, like many prophets, they did not always come off, for something like an atomic war was expected very soon after His death. The error may well have been due to the difficulty of interpreting the passage of time, which is experienced by many fortune tellers today.

Dunne worked out an extremely complicated explanation of this strange phenomenon. The explanation, which did not seem to make the question any easier to understand, tended to obscure the basic fact. Time did not always go on ticking in one direction for ever. Sometimes it ticked backwards and effect came before cause. The egg was there before the hen laid it; the man was killed by the bullet before it hit him and so on.

Whatever the explanation of this phenomenon may be, it will not be obtained by denying the facts. Too many have found future elements in their dreams for that attitude to be considered. We have to admit that these apparently impossible things occur, and then see whether there is not some relatively simple, natural explanation to account for them.

Over and above everything else there appears to be an external system and we have only touched the fringes of it. This system seems to be so detailed that it is possible to recognise the food plant of a particular insect by the length of cord on a pendulum and the number of times it rotates. It is possible to trace the movements of a person round the world, observe when he is ill, and appreciate the part of his body affected. We have by divination also learnt of the accident to a friend, fifteen miles away, three hours before that accident took place. This appears incredible, but it is all down in my notebook. We are dealing all the time with the apparently impossible and there must be some natural reason for the results.

All these measurements and experiments took years to perform and there is probably no limit to what you could find out. We have one fixed point in this problem, which is that dreams often contain elements drawn from future time. This cannot be evaded. Dunne tried to get round it, but not very convincingly. The explanation must be quite simple and not need an elaborate system of observers. A possible answer is that this earth life is not real and we are now going over something which has been lived already. If this were so, then it would perhaps be possible to go into the place where the film was projected and look over it for both forward and backward shots (just as you can unroll a cinema film and examine it when it is not being shown). Could this be what happens when we go to sleep? Do we just go into the projection room and look over the film? If so there must be an infinite number of people looking over an infinite number of films at the same time.

If we take this idea and examine the flash and strip types of dream, there appears to be some confirmation. So many of them seem to resemble the results of people trying out stills and little strips of film on projectors of some kind. They often appear to do it inexpertly and shots stick or come on back to front.

If there is any truth in this idea, it could begin to give us remarkable thoughts of what may be happening in the next zone, for it suggests that there may be mechanical projectors there not very different from those we know here. This is a long way from the old idea of people sitting on wet clouds and twanging harps, yet it seems to be a more practical possibility.

I have seen a large number of stills of people and there are several strange points about them. They are like ordinary earth pictures (photographs, drawings or paintings). They are always strangers. There are others of dogs, but never of dogs the dreamer remembers. There are stills which can be appreciated as coming from photographs or postcards. When seeing these you get exactly the same impression as when watching somebody operating some form of projector. There is a yet more remarkable point. Two of my stills did not come on properly. One stuck in the left corner and I could not see the whole face. The other came more than half way on and there stopped with a hard blank end just as if a lantern slide had stuck in the 'gate'. I feel reasonably certain that these were indeed lantern slides. If so where and how are they being put on? Who is doing it? Other people often tell me that they have dreams of this kind.

Are we seeing projections taking place in the next zone, on some private type of television projector? If so (and people will call me crazy for making the suggestion) these stills might be call-up signs to attract the attention of a particular person.

Obviously if these things are call-ups, then it is only by chance that we happen to see them. We perhaps are changing our rate of vibration from sleeping to waking, or back again, and for an instant happen to be on the right length to pick up a particular sign. An alternative possibility appears to be that (since there is no time in the next zone) when we get there in sleep, we may be able to pick up transmissions from some form of apparatus not yet produced on earth.

Of course either of these suggestions must be highly tentative, yet it seems possible that having got so far something may come along to add to our information. What is needed is a considerable number of people collecting their dreams over a long time. Then, if these were brought together and worked over, quite a lot of facts would emerge.

By using the pendulum we can somehow obtain a great deal of information on many subjects, which cannot be obtained through our normal five senses. Is there any clue in the dreams, which might give us a hint as to whether we are dealing with some possible future state, or with one merely on a higher rate of vibration?

There is one on which I do not really trust my own observation; first, because the space of time in which I can use it is too short and second because my mind is muzzy with sleep when it takes place. However, I do think that the people whom I observe for short periods in the flash dreams are not dressed in a fashion which might suggest that they lived at some future time. The dress of both men and women and the hair styles of the latter, do not appear very much different from what I have known. However, one might think that in some cases they were rather out of date; but in no case have I been surprised by them. Fashion is changing so fast that it seems unlikely that these pictures belong to a time even thirty years ahead of today. I think that they are contemporary, or often a little earlier. I have not seen yet one of the lank hair styles common in what is already known as the 'Age of Ugly Women', by which the present years are designated. Therefore my impression is that I usually see pictures of people who lived between perhaps 1900 and 1960. As I say, I do not trust this, but it may be of some importance.

In Graham Tidman's dream (see Appendix, dream 10) a whole sequence of events appears to have been locked up in the house itself. (I shall mention how we demonstrated by throwing stones at a wall that you could lock something of your personality up in them and subsequently detect it with a pendulum.) We are already prepared by Mrs Beresford's experience with the budgerigar for events to be passed into somebody else's dream before they happen. Graham Tidman did come here in the end and make contact with the place. Therefore it appears that his dreams were really due to his picking the correct vibrations out of the place when he came here, but they were moved forward in time in the dreams. Of course this is impossible in earth time, but it does not seem to be so in dream time.

Equally puzzling is my dream of the unknown officer of the Rifles (see Appendix, dream 33) walking down the road with a basket on his arm to play a game in some unknown place. The actual event must have taken place long before I was born. This could certainly be called a ghost experience. But I did not dream it in the locality where it must have taken place. I had the dream here in our bedroom. No one alive could have communicated it to me by telepathy. The first idea is that it could have come to me from the room itself, in which it had been implanted long ago by someone's memory. The second is that when going to sleep I had passed through a zone where a film of this particular series of incidents was being projected. It might have formed part of a historical lecture, or something of that kind. This suggestion would appear to be utterly fantastic had we not had numerous examples of the same kind of thing in the flash dreams. In those we continually find something, which looks like lantern slide projection. We do not know where it is going on but we guess that it takes place in a zone of vibration higher than the one in which we are living. If by any chance this is the correct explanation, then we have to infer the existence of another zone, not unlike this but perhaps a little more evolved, in which people make use of apparatus for teaching, or other purposes, not dissimilar to that in use here. Is this particularly improbable? I think it is only improbable if you are so wedded to materialistic thought that you are not capable of imagining any form of survival of bodily death. If the human mind does survive bodily death and go on evolving, then what we seem to be finding out about the next zone appears to be completely reasonable. Many people would surely wish to widen their knowledge in a way similar to that practised in the zone from which they came.

I have not had anything to do with spiritualism but I have read a number of books purporting to have been handed down to mediums by people now living on a higher (or faster) zone. I cannot help noticing many resemblances between what is reported in these books and what we appear to be learning from our study of dreams. The statements of the one branch of study tend to confirm the findings of the other.

However, we must remain obstinately curious in all this study. When everything is so nebulous it is only too easy to believe anything which looks like making sense. I think it is clear from working over the dreams that our imagination does add to some extent to what is actually dreamt.

Man exists on many mental levels, of which the earth life appears to be the lowest. On this level he gathers information to be used by his real self on levels above. He is not an animal but is compelled to use an animal body to be able to exist on the low level. He is not the equal of any other man. He is entirely independent and his method of development is peculiar to himself. On this level he is completely alone and all his decisions are his own, to forward his own development. Only when he can realise this will he rise at all in the scale of evolution. Higher in the scale he is probably not so much alone.

If you find out anything, I feel it is your duty to pass it on to your fellows. So although I know many will snort contemptuously at what I have written, I also know that it was my duty to write it. It is their loss and not mine. They can be as happy as they can in their rat race and greed for gain but in the end they will learn that they have missed something far more important. You cannot buy your social status on the higher levels; you have to earn it by enlarging your mental capacity, and in this mental capacity is power.

The power is yours on the higher level (power to heal, power to help and power to find out things unknown), but to make use of it here, it is necessary to learn how it can be brought down to a lower level. The transformer is something which you forge mentally between one level and the next and it looks as if the force which operates it is known as bio-electronics (living electricity).

There is value in a collection of facts, even if you cannot see at once what they indicate. It is more than likely that the conclusions which I have suggested can be shown to be completely wrong; but there can be no harm in making them and giving other people something to think about, even if it ends in their wanting to throw empty bottles at me. It does occur to me to wonder how many people there are who are in the position to throw a bottle, and even then whether they could hit the target.

5   Types of Dreams

The Reversed Dream

It seems as if our research work with dowsing and the pendulum may throw quite a lot of light on this curious problem. Although nobody really knows how the mind works, yet there is no reason to suppose that it ever runs completely backwards in time. Still, it is quite clear that something happens in dreams, which gives the impression that it does this very action. We can assume that this is not some kind of illusion and must have a rational explanation. I am not sure that I have found the correct answer; neither may I be capable of explaining what I think may happen; but I will try to do so.

If an object is placed on the ground (for example a piece of silver, which has a pendulum rate of 22 inches) the observer can approach this object from any direction, with the pendulum set for this 22 inch rate, and, when he reaches a distance of 22 inches from the object, the pendulum will rotate 22 times. This appears to be the constant signature for silver. On the same 22 inch rate, lead will make the pendulum revolve 18 times, sodium 30 times and calcium 36 times. There is thus a circle of 22 inches radius round a silver object in which the pendulum acts as I have said. This circle can be shown to be the base of two conjoined very narrow cones extending vertically upwards and downwards.

Now it can be further demonstrated that there is a false position for the piece of silver 62 inches from the observer and on a straight line produced from the one joining him to the object. Wherever he stands on the edge of the first circle, he will find a false position for the piece of silver opposite and over five feet distant. These false positions have each in turn another 22 inch circle round them. The false position lies exactly where it ought to do if it lay in its correct place on the spiral of rates on the second whorl. If you were looking for silver on the plane above sleep and death, this is where you would find it. But these two circles do not touch at their circumference and this difference is presumably proportionate to the angle of climb of the spiral. Whatever the cause may be, it seems to show that there is some displacement zone between the two apparent positions of the object which might be compared with the known refraction which occurs between air and water. Thought images of events can be shown to obey these conditions also. Determination, for instance, has the same 22 inch rate as silver.

Now the rate for sleep is 40 inches and so presumably dreams are beyond this number and on the second whorl of the spiral. Because of this displacement zone, they are bound to be to some extent different from whatever caused them on the waking earth level. However important this may be, this is not the point I am trying to make. We are trying to see why pictures of incidents should come on back to front.

There is time affecting everything on earth and this is presumed to run in a straight line from birth to death. Of course this may not be a correct assumption. Its course too may be a spiral one. But we will assume that it is so and everything moves in a straight line in time. Now on the second whorl there is no time. This is very hard to understand but I think we must take it that (as the pendulum shows us) although there is no time there is still the sequence of events. If so they will radiate out in every direction, on the correct rate, from the point at which they reached the second whorl. From the point of view of the observer travelling on his straight time path, some sequences will run backwards in reversed order and others forward in the correct order. He is moving, they are static. Whether he gets a reversed dream, a normal progression, or a mixed one, probably depends on the degree of awareness which he retains when passing into or out of the second whorl (Figure 5, p.78). If he happens to notice the backward sequence more than the forward one, he will return to earth with a dream like the cat coming into a room backwards, or a horse jumping a fence hind legs first. There is nothing unreasonable, or unnatural about this. However, it is rather a relief to know that the second whorl is not the end of everything and that there is a third one on which the time sequence returns again and even a similar fourth one above that. There is probably no end to this sequence, but death is only found between the earth level and the second level.

Future Dreams

Suppose that the observer travels from his point on earth up to the point which is his displaced position on the second whorl. Down below (of course it is not necessarily down below at all, but it is convenient to speak of it like that) events move on in time on their steady path. But where the observer is there is no time, yet there is sequence. He may well watch the events of days in a flash, turn over newspapers, watch the television, anything. Then quite suddenly something catches his eye, something shocking, or alarming perhaps. He wakes up with a start, a long way ahead in time from where he started. Much of the sequence he has been watching has not yet happened in earth time; although it has in the 'no time' sequence where he was. He may have appreciated something which was days, or weeks, ahead in earth time.

This is a problem far beyond anything we usually encounter. At a given point on another mind level, you can appreciate events which have not yet happened. You can read the headlines of a newspaper, which will not be printed for days ahead. But you are not in earth life when you do so. You are beyond the point of sleep and of death (both are 40 inches in rate). This is a most drastic piece of information. Does it mean that time on earth is also an illusion and everything really happens in a flash? Does it mean that events on earth are no more than a projection from the next levels forced on to a moving time belt? Is there any way of changing them? It is not my business to answer these questions. I am only trying to deal with facts. But it does seem to me that it must be impossible to change events which you read of in a newspaper dream days before the thing is printed. It is the old question of which came first, the egg or the chicken? If anyone knows the answer, it may be in the learning of some Tibetan sage; but it certainly is not known to the religious men of the Western world. I think perhaps if you dream you are driving a car over a cliff, it might be as well to avoid driving near one for a time; but I do not think that that really is the way to look at it, because there is some evident distortion in dreams. The thing to do must be to try to find out more about the second and third whorls of the spiral.

One finds all this in the sayings of the fortune tellers. They get some things right and some slightly distorted. They are also often most uncertain whether an event has happened already, or is yet to come. Gypsies were often very fond of gold coins. Some had ancient and valuable specimens. I have told in another book (*Ghost and Ghoul,* p.76) how a gypsy woman once came to my house in Cambridge and asked for a gold coin, which she was convinced that I had. She would not believe that there was no such coin in the house. The coin was found many years later in Devon. She had got her dating confused owing to the absence of time on the next level whence she drew her information somehow.

This absence of time on one whorl and its presence on others, is a fundamental matter and until it is understood the errors in dreams and foretelling the future will remain inexplicable. Now, however, that we can begin to get our information collected in diagrammatic form, it should become easier to understand. No doubt there will be mistakes in my attempts at explanation; but it is open to anybody to write down his dreams and examine them for himself and it is also possible for at least half mankind to experiment with the pendulum. (The idea that few can be dowsers is wrong.)

The picture that seems to be forming is not utterly unlike Dunne's theory of serialism. There appears to be a series of observers (if you can so describe a succession of degrees of mental awareness) but they are not exact counterparts of the original observer. The time succession is quite unlike his, for the second observer finds himself on a mental plane where there is succession but no movement of time. On the third plane, time begins to move once more. It seems possible that the Roman Catholic idea of Purgatory originated in some knowledge of what appears to happen on the second timeless whorl. The more one looks into these subjects, the clearer it becomes that far back in the Ages men knew much more about them than they do today. One has only to look at the teachings of Jesus, Buddha and the Kahunas to see that this must be so.

It is hard to visualise what happens on the second plane. But perhaps it is not particularly inept to picture each particular incident as a stone thrown into quiet water with ripples spreading out in all directions (see Figure 5). There will be an infinite number of these points and the ripples will have no troughs between them. The earth level time will pass through a particular point in a straight line; whichever way it passes through, it will hit the same successions. However, some will go forward and some backward. If you happen to concentrate on the backward ripples, you will return from sleep with an impression of things moving backwards. However, if you concentrate on the forward series, you will at first get ordinary memories of events which have already happened in earth time and then, as the point on the second level does not move, you will receive impressions of things which have not yet happened.

Whether the second-level impressions are more true than those on the earth plane is difficult to decide. A little way back we had a hint that telepathy at any rate operated on this level. If this is right, then telepathic dreams must pass from the second level to the earth plane and so perhaps all do. The impact of the stone on the water may be spread out in earth time so that we can learn more from what we appreciate. Although this is all most difficult to understand, yet it has to be explained somehow and for the moment I can get no further with it. We must not forget there is a third level above the second on which time moves on again once more. There is even a fourth level above this, where once more moving time appears to exist. Of course the term 'level' is not correct. It would be more exact to speak of whorls of the spiral. Their number may be unlimited, yet we have as yet only found evidence of one (the second) on which time is static. On this one too there is no response to death at 80 inches although there is for black on the same rate.

Therefore the second whorl appears to differ very greatly from the one on which our minds normally appear to function. Although reds, greens and blues are still there and silver is still silver, there is no apparent passing of time and there is no need for you to go to sleep or die on it before moving on to the third. Of course I am only getting this information from the pendulum; but numerous other experimenters are now beginning to get similar results to mine and at least at one point there appears to be a link with orthodox science. For instance what brings beetles into a lighted room? (See Appendix, dream 4.)

Three months after I had started noting down dreams Mr E. H. S. Van Someren of Cambridge very kindly sent me four offprints by Philip S. Callagan, recently published by the Entomological Society of America. These are highly technical reports and theories dealing with the flight of insects to their food supply and to their mates. The title of one of them will be enough to give some idea of how specialised these articles are: 'Insect molecular bioelectronics: a theoretical and experimental study of insect sensillae as tubular waveguides, with particular emphasis on their dielectric and thermoelectric properties.' Readers need not be unduly alarmed. I have no intention of making anything but the shortest précis of Mr Callagan's most important work (much of which is entirely above my head and probably also above the heads of most of the insect specialists in the USA).

As far as I can understand it Callagan has gone a long way beyond Fabre's theory that insects are drawn to their food and to one another by unsmellable smells. These unsmellable scents come into his theories but only in the last stages of the attraction. The main pull (and that over long distances) is comparable to radar. The wing beats of the insect are thought to generate enough heat to produce the electricity necessary to send out a vibration, which contacts the required object. When the insect has flown down this beam to within a relatively short distance of its objective a second built-in reaction to scent waves brings it dead on target. The technical details of the whole elaborate process are of no importance here; the point is that it seems to be unmistakably the same as that which has been deduced from the study of the behaviour of insects by using the pendulum. The pendulum also appears to demonstrate the existence of a numerological scheme at the back of all these vibrations. For the first time we begin to see direct links between so-called magic and orthodox science. When followed to its logical conclusions the effect of this on thinking can only be enormous. An ordered world governed by unseen vibrations will take the place of the materialism of today. Somebody must have planned the numbers. No chance could have arranged that *Chrysomela methrasti* for example should have the same pendulum rate and number of rotations as its food plant, mint (*mentha*). This similarity can be observed in many species. Presumably the insect obtains this built-in radar reaction in the first place from the plant on which it feeds in infancy, but going beyond that point, what decided that a given substance should have a particular notation?

Is not this something which really appears to have been known for nearly two thousand years? Why otherwise was Jesus reported as saying 'The very hairs of your head are numbered'? I am convinced that very much knowledge has been lost through the ages and sometimes distorted out of all recognition. We are slowly beginning to learn it all again.

6   Pendulum Rates

For long ages and all over the world it is curious how men have believed that there were higher beings who watched over what they did. Why should they have thought this? You may say that men are not stupid and throughout their lives some have observed a kind of plan. From their observations they naturally assumed that someone, whom they could not see, had contrived it. When you look at the recently recovered beliefs of the Polynesian Kaundas, you must see that this is not the answer. They knew that there was a method of getting in touch with what they called their higher self, who was much more powerful than they were and could help them when in trouble. I have not gone into this at all fully but it seems to fit in with what we can learn with our code and the pendulum. I must try to explain the code in greater detail, for the Kaundas not only had a higher self, they also had a lower one. They seem to have known about both superconscious and subconscious mind levels.

So far I have touched only on the pendulum's activities in relation to chemical elements on our earth level. However, once you appreciate that you are dealing with some unstudied subject outside the ordinary run of scientific research, you will realise that the established bounds of earth study do not apply to it. From this point the whole quest expands and you begin to see that you can find pendulum co-ordinates for mental concepts, which are not concrete at all. You see that a concept of a clock on the wall is no more concrete than one of indignation when you tread on a drawing pin. It becomes perfectly easy to find the rate and number of gyrations belonging to anger or satisfaction, to memory or dishonesty. All that needs to be done is to think of the concept and unwind the gently swinging pendulum until it gyrates. Absurdly simple though this appears to be, it can be tested repeatedly giving the same result.

Naturally no one trained in the old style can possibly believe any of this without testing it for himself. Unfortunately it is clear that those likely to be the least credulous have not the potential to work the pendulum; while in many others the potential is so low that it takes considerable practice before they can get reasonable results. The potential can be developed. I have a friend in whom it was once very low but who is now efficient in using the pendulum. There are a few people too in whom the potential is not only low but negative. Why this should be the case I have no means of finding out. They are sometimes the very persons who would most like to take part in the investigation.

When we have collected a large number of pendulum rates it is possible to look at them like any other collection—stamps, fossils, or what you will—and get them into some kind of order. As it happens I have rather a dislike of decimals and find metric scales arbitrary. Therefore I measured all rates in inches (since inches, feet and yards have a natural basis). All our pendulum rates are found in a table of 40 inches; true East, South, West and North have the rates of 10, 20, 30 and 40. At once our rates become part of something to do with the solid earth itself and not of its magnetic field as many have assumed. Of course these rates are not exact, for each thought ray has a width of two inches.

Having now recognised our cardinal points, it is instructive to make a circular card of forty divisions and put our rates each on the appropriate ray of this card, which is in reality a form of compass rose. This rose is full of information; but the most important facts cluster on the spokes up to the cardinal points. For instance on 40 inches we find north, anger, sleep, death, cold, black and other concepts, mostly of an unpleasant nature. How could these rates possibly have got there, unless the whole thing was planned? Perhaps one might consider the idea that the arrangement might be the product of our own unconscious mind, but this is not so. Other people, experimenting with different apparatus, get the same figures. Some years ago I found the rate for general health between 31 and 33 inches. I call it 32 inches. A little time later I read a book by Dr Ash in which he described finding the health rate, varying between 31 and 32 inches, by elaborate apparatus. His methods were so entirely different that one is convinced that there really is a rate for general health and that it is 32 inches. Who decided this?

It would be easy to write numerous books about these rates and the compass rose which they form. However, this would be quite outside what we are looking for. It is interesting to find that male is not (as we have always been brought up to think) the opposite of female. From their positions on the card at 24 and 29 inches, one would fancy that whether a person is male or female has little importance in the superconscious mind. But many opposites are informative and so are the groupings on various numbers. Look at 22 inches: the colour grey is 22:7 and the metals, lead 22:16, silver 22:22, calcium 22:30 and sodium 22:36 are all on the same rate. The colour blue and the metal cobalt share one also. Think for a moment about the curious grouping on 29 inches. There is female and gold, which for millennia females have desired for ornament. There is the yellow of the gold and there is danger. Is there a connection between femininity and danger (the female of the species is more deadly than the male perhaps); or is there some other explanation, for yellow plants are frequently poisonous?

These observations could be endless. Grass is 16 inches. Grass which has passed through cows and horses, appearing again as dung, is 16 inches; while the beetles of the Scarab family, which feed on and spend their lives in that dung, are also on the 16 inch rate. Then beside these first three, whose connection is obvious, we find evolution and can see no reason why it should be there. Its opposite, devolution, is on 36 inches, where one would expect to find it; while on 16 inches there is sex itself as opposed to male and female.

Of course I am trying to reason from far too little information. Where I have perhaps two hundred rates, there must be thousands, if not millions. Where I have two co-ordinates (rate and gyration count) there must be dozens.

Nevertheless I have many of the more important mental conceptions. Even the four cardinal points and such things as life and death, sun and moon, red and green and so on are enough to make us think. Why are they numbered and who numbered them? 'The very hairs of your head are numbered', Jesus said and to this the pendulum replied: 'Yes, they have a rate of eleven and a half inches.' This is not meant to be blasphemous; it is an observed fact. As it happens we have the rates for most parts of the body. Yet with mischievous and even evil people using magic today, it is advisable not to spread these numbers about too generally.

It is clear that as the number of known rates increases, they soon become too many for one card. Still, the circular form is very convenient and so it is advisable to construct several cards. A still more interesting situation can be seen if, instead of just writing the rates anywhere up their appropriate spoke within a circle, you measure the actual length of the rate up that spoke. Of course you will not do this on the full natural scale. A 40 inch disc is a large object and it is handy to reduce it to quarter size. Now that you have your 10 inch disc and its forty spokes you mark the rates of the thought concepts at a quarter of their true length. Join each point so produced to the next one on the nearest spoke and soon you see that instead of a circle you have a flat spiral. This is another vital clue in our study.

I made my first spiral of rates and sat looking at it. There is something fascinating about a spiral and many forms of life are constructed on its plan. More than half the empty shells you pick up idly on the beach are spirals. If you look at the sawn end of a tree trunk, there is a spiral of yearly ring growth. People have suggested often that all life develops as a spiral and time repeats sequences from whorl to whorl. I had not expected to find a spiral of rates.

As I had drawn it out, the spiral ended at 40 inches. There was the cold north pole and there was death. I should, so far as our research work had gone, have ended there. But I found it hard to believe that this was the right answer. The figure looked as if it was incomplete. I could think of nothing in nature, which simply produced a single spiral whorl and then stopped abruptly. A spiral is a growing and expanding concept and not just a blank twist of wire. Probably I was only being imaginative but it seemed to me that the spiral ought to go on. It might expand with the same regularity as that with which it started, or it might turn back on itself. Whatever it did, I did not think it had finished (Figure 3).

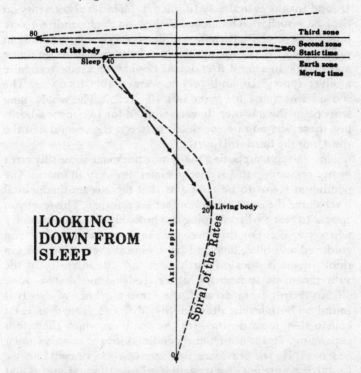

Figure 3 This diagram attempts to show how the Spiral of Rates explains why people in dreams, or during 'out of the body' experiences, can look down on their body from above and to one side of it. The second whorl of the spiral may have no thickness, or be of unlimited extent. From sleep at 40, the dreamer looks at himself at 20.

It did not appear to be difficult to make sure of this. If the spiral continued as a second, or even a third whorl, then there would presumably be rates for objects on these whorls, even though the state of the concepts involved was beyond the point of death. Experiment showed that this was indeed the case. Each thought form had a second rate on a second whorl of the spiral; but there were a few notable exceptions. One of the most important of these was time.

When confronted with a problem of this kind, one looks around for the easiest way to solve it. Metals had been easy on the first whorl; what happened to them on the second? We were looking beyond 40, the point of death on the first whorl. If an object then had a rate on the second whorl, it must surely be appreciable to a mind after death? Could such a mind recognise a silver spoon? Undoubtedly it seemed able to do so. The second whorl rate for silver was 40+22:22. The whole thing worked in this manner. It even worked for two more whorls; but there was no rate for death between the second and the third, nor the third and fourth.

Now, always supposing that I have not made some silly error in my reasoning, this is surely something very dramatic. The pendulum seems to be telling us that there is another mental level above the one to which we are accustomed. This level you appear to reach when sleeping and probably go to permanently when you die. On this level the mind appreciates silver and gold, red and blue, love and light, almost everything you can think of, as it does on earth; although the intensity of the appreciation is apparently higher. Judging by what we have already learnt from dreams, the same sequence of events is found on both levels; although they differ to some degree. Of course they must do this, for the spiral on which they lie is expanding. This is not Dunne's endless series of exactly similar observers. He was reasoning that time was on a straight line. We find that we are not on a straight line but on a spiral, and as that spiral grows, so must the observer change, and so must the sequence change.

There is a puzzle, as one might expect, about time and the spiral. It is at first rather a shock to be unable to find a rate for it on the earth whorl. We use the concept of time continuously on this level. Why is it not there? The answer seems to be that time is, on this particular level, always running away from the pendulum and you cannot pin it down and rate it. But on the next level up you find it easily. It is 40+20.

Now if our earth time is moving on a straight line, the time on the next mental level must be something quite different. It is not moving at all. But there is a sequence on this second level and so there must be many series of events stored somehow on it. Since we experience these sequences in dreams, it is clear that they can be put on to a moving time scale, just as one can put a cinema film on to a projector; but until this is done they are meaningless and inert. It seems to me that a sequence on the second mind level must be represented not by a line like a ruler but by a dot. I visualise each sequence as an infinitesimally small globe composed of what we must call 'onion skins' of experience.

I think it must be clear now what we are finding. These dots are memories. Our second mental whorl on the spiral becomes a vast library of memories. The memories are not tied to our earth time and so 'future' events can be revealed but, owing to the expanding of the spiral, they will not correspond exactly with what happens on earth. More than this, we can see from a study of dreams that these memories in the library are available in some telepathic manner to people other than those who experience the sequences which the memories store.

One would expect this to be the end of it all and assume that after death a person just browses in a vast storehouse of memories until it becomes such a bore that he cannot be bothered to continue his existence. However, the pendulum shows that this idea is wrong. There is a third whorl above the second and a fourth above the third and on both these whorls time is as it is on earth. You walk out of the museum into a new life of time and sequence. I say 'walk' because the pendulum indicates that there is no death beyond the first one.

I think we must assume that when we experience memories during earth life, we have already got a foot on the second level. The memories come to us by chance and in no particular order. We have just taken a particular dot out of the collection, which some incident in earth life has brought to our notice. We can even do it deliberately. The block between the two levels is not very solid.

Many races have taught that after death a person has to review his past earth life. It seems that this may well be the truth; although we have no means of telling whether there is any compulsion to do so. The Roman Catholic Church with its teaching of Purgatory seems to be pretty close to the truth. In any case the second level is not your future life. It is simply a level on which your past life can be studied in detail and notes taken on what has been done well or badly. There is no set time on it, for presumably each individual will wish to spend a different period going over his records.

If you can use a pendulum, or divining rod, you can demonstrate so many facts to your own satisfaction that you can think things out for yourself. You build up your own faith by your own work. I did not believe in any of this when I first started the investigation of divining. Each time a new fact comes along I doubt it and often go back to doubting the whole subject; but it will not be denied. If you can find unknown concrete objects again and again when they are completely concealed, it becomes impossible to doubt; and what can be checked for some facts can often be checked for others. The result is not faith but conviction. You are convinced by your results. In faith you have to accept what you are told and this does not appear to be particularly good for your mental evolution; it is shutting a door on a faculty which you are given to use: curiosity. So, if you can work the pendulum and are not too lazy to spend considerable time in using it, there is nothing to prevent you from finding out all the facts I have mentioned and many more besides. We are just at the start of what appears to be a science embracing all sciences known today. But to be pioneers in this work you need to have a completely open mind; faith is the last thing you want, for it excludes any possibility of using your powers of reasoning from observed fact.

Psi Potential

I really became involved in this study from two completely different angles, both of which began with archaeology. It was impossible to avoid an investigation of ancient religions, because I found evidence relating to some of them. I became interested in divining, first through the chance seeing of ghosts, and then from curiosity to find out how such things took place. If you could induce ghosts at will, as many apparently do by psychometry, you could learn much about ancient civilisation and so on. Was it a practicable possibility? Was it archaeology?

These two lines of research were so utterly different that there seemed to be very little chance of finding any link between them. In fact links are numerous. Before long I realised that most of the subjects known as supernatural, occult, parapsychological and so on, were all aspects of one study. If one was shown to exist, all of them did. All were linked up with dreams, memories, magic and hypnosis, fortune telling, psychometry and telepathy. All tended towards (although it was forcefully denied) religious beliefs held by mankind through the ages. The materialists, of course, did not believe in any of it; but then the pendulum study showed that many of them had such a low potential that they were the equivalent of colour blind and could not experience much of it anyhow.

This potential, whatever it may really be, is generally known as 'psi' and a person's psi count can be worked out with the pendulum set at 9½ inches. In practice it is found that a person whose number of gyrations at 9½ inches is under ten, will have some difficulty in using the pendulum or divining rod; with repeated experiments the number can apparently be steadily increased. Whether we can equate psi with intuition is not certain; but it seems probable that intuition is a facet of the larger psi.

A certain number of people have no psi count but instead react to a minus rating of 29½ inches. As far as we can judge at present this minus reading is combined with, or due to, some nervous disability. There is also a sex rate at 16 inches, which is distinct from the rates for male and female. The normal count for sex is somewhere between 16 and 20 turns. It has been observed that persons who have a high sex rate of over 40 turns are liable to have a very low psi count. This is not invariable; nor is it the case that a low sex count is always found with a high psi. However, the pendulum does suggest that too much preoccupation with sex is liable to deaden the more intuitive faculties. One could hardly be expected to find any other result; although many great artists have not been celebrated for their moderation in this matter. The name of Benvenuto Cellini comes into one's mind at once; famous as he became both for his art and his sex life.

To return to psi. In the last few years it has become clear that there is no great gulf fixed between orthodox experiment using electronic techniques and an unorthodox one employing the primitive instruments of long ago. Actually there is a great saving in trouble, time and expense if the latter are employed. The child's cotton reel on a thread tells the same story as the most elaborate piece of electronic apparatus. Of course mankind is so perverse that it will prefer to spend much money on the latter to taking a little trouble to master the former. 'The expert must know best.' But does he? And why is he an expert? Actually his subject is very recent; while nearly two thousand years ago Christ taught that unless you became again as a little child you could not really advance. This had an upsetting effect on Nicodemus, who was an expert in those far-off days, but he did make some attempt to understand, which is more than can be said of many of our present-day specialists.

It is by paying attention to animals that we can get perhaps a better idea of how psi works than by looking at our neighbours. With animals psi still functions as it is meant to do, for their minds remain unhampered by long ethical training of one kind or another. Each one is out for himself and no nonsense. Cats are the least 'civilised' of the domestic animals; but they certainly have a sense of friendship and of humour. However, to think that you own a cat is ridiculous. It owns you and on occasion, with great kindness on its part, it will bring you a mouse, mole or bird as a present; particularly if it knows by its psi that you are worried or unwell.

The cat's psi is a most efficient and unexpected faculty. Although their eyesight is not good in daytime and they find it difficult to distinguish stationary objects unless they convert them into moving pictures by rapidly sliding their eyes from side to side, they have a way of locating things which is far superior to any of our normal five senses. Of course dogs have it too and, being less selfish, are more ready to make use of it to help human beings. I think the cat's private radar seems more efficient. It is noticeable too that it works very well when they are asleep, which apparently indicates that, like human beings, they live on other whorls of the spiral. It would seem that the cat is as immortal as the Pope, or the Archbishop of Canterbury; though I doubt whether they would be pleased to have this proved to them.

We have a Siamese cat and this almost completely wild animal is a great hunter. On most mornings before we get up she comes into the bedroom and goes to sleep on the end of the bed. One morning she sat up with a jerk and began to scan the corner of the room. She seemed to fix a bearing, jumped off the bed and ran out of the open door. In about three minutes she was back with a short-tailed field vole, which she devoured with horrid noises under the bed.

Now, on her line of bearing, there is a grassy bank beside the lane, about twenty-five yards from where she was sleeping. To get there she had to run along a passage in the opposite direction, across a big bedroom, down the backstairs, across the kitchen, out of the window, through a small court, round two sides of the house and then across a yard. It seemed clear that she had picked up the position of the vole in her sleep and then fixed this on her waking mind. At least two mental levels were involved. She kept that bearing in her mind through several changes in direction and knew exactly where the vole was. It had no chance of escape. This has happened several times since then, and the same revolting ritual feast has taken place beneath our bed.

It seemed probable that the cat's whiskers acted like divining rods and I decided to try and find out their co-ordinates in our pendulum code. There is more work in this than anyone might think, for not only have you to rate the whiskers but you have to find out to what thought forms these co-ordinates also belong. Actually the cat has at least four sets of bristles. The longest and furthest back have a rate of 16 inches for sex, which is not a surprise. The next group is on 20 inches. Man comes on this rate, with love and life. The smallest and farthest forward of the groups is on 24 inches. On this rate you also find mice. Finally, its eyebrows are on 10 inches. On 10 inches you also find heat, explaining surely how a cat knows with unerring certainty where to find the warmest spot in the house.

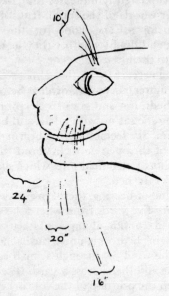

Figure 4   Diagram of a cat's face to show the rates of its whiskers as indicated by the pendulum: 10″=heat and light; 16″=sex; 20″=living things and man; 24″=mammals.

These four groups of bristles, then, seem to explain a cat's vigorous sex life; its fondness for mankind; its passion for mice and its love of warmth (Figure 4). This can hardly be either chance or coincidence, but looks like a carefully planned arrangement. If you were asked to describe the characteristics of a cat, surely these four would come high on your list. One cannot avoid the thought that some creator considered that a cat would be a useful thing for man to have about the house. If you add the remarkable beauty of a Siamese cat, you might also think that the very sight of one would be thought good for man's artistic evolution. Perhaps I am writing complete nonsense, but if you think so, explain how chance evolution from a little lump of jelly produced the picture. Man soon needed a hunting friend to keep the vermin out of his shelter. The Greeks even tried taming pine-martens for this purpose. However, the cat fitted the bill exactly. Still, it is a terribly sexy beast and produced so many kittens that, unlike the dog, it won no rights in the laws of the land. In Wales they were more sensible and the man who killed a royal cat had to produce a wergild of enough corn to cover it completely when the corpse was held up by the tail with its nose on the floor. This must surely have been at least a hundredweight of grain.

7 Bio-Electronics

Of course cats are not the only beasts with whiskers and obviously not unique in their radar system. But they are easy to observe and give many people the chance to check their observations. There seems to be little reason to suppose that their psi operates in a way different from our own. If a cat knows where another is when it is fast asleep, presumably our minds work in a similar way. It uses bristles to locate hidden things; we use a divining rod to find underground water. Then it seems reasonable to infer that our divining rod or pendulum takes us into the realm of sleep; and, since we are not provided with bristles in the same degree as a cat, we need artificial aids to get information back from there. The information is not available on the earth level of mind at all. Apparently the higher-level minds know it all and can, one thinks, probably see hidden things, because things which we can sense here (such as colours and metals) are provided with rates on the pendulum and so apparently must exist on the next level also. The general idea is not difficult to grasp but the mechanics of it are not those of the ordinary three-dimensional world and this is upsetting to the materialistic mind. However, here we can now begin to see the possibility of a shift in thinking.

My readers are frequently kind and helpful, putting before me information which I would not otherwise have obtained. I have talked about this shift at some length in *The Monkey's Tail* and will not go into it much here. The point is that P. Callagan, researching in the USA and using elaborate electronic apparatus, was able to find out how moths located distant food plants and their mates, flying down to them on beams, or rays.

The current needed to produce what Callagan called bio-electronic rays was generated by the heat caused by the vibration of their wings, and the organs employed in this were bristles.

While Callagan was doing his research, it happened that I was working with a pendulum on beetles and their food plants. It appeared that the genus *Chrysomela* was linked to the botanical order of *Labiatae*. When tested it was shown that a particular species had the same rate and number of gyrations as the species of food plant on which it had been reared. There was no question of a small insect flying aimlessly about the countryside and hoping to find something nice to eat. It knew exactly where that food plant was by its radar. The dung beetle knew where to find dung. Thanks to P. Callagan we can now see that the cat gets its information through a stone wall by bio-electronic rays and, since these can be measured by orthodox scientific instruments, we are no longer in the realm of magic. Nor does it seem possible that chance had any part in the story. Surely someone must have arranged that a given beetle eats a given plant and in so doing builds the rate and count of that plant into its own structure. This is planning of a high order. Think of the processes which are involved (chemical, electronic, genetic, mental, aerodynamic, and more besides) before an *Aphodius* beetle can fly direct to a cowpat in my field; and how long would it have taken it, wandering through the grass roots, to find that cowpat without its bio-electronic radar? When we come to the *Chrysomelidae*, some of the species are quite rare and so are the food plants. The chances of success without the radar would be so small that many beetles would never have a meal at all and the species would die out.

Of course we do not know what this higher mind is, because we are only the products of its thinking; but the pendulum does give us one clue. There is apparently no time on the second whorl of the spiral and so to a mind, which operates on that level, there need not be eons of time between each experiment. They could be carried out when and for as long as the Creator remained interested. As soon as that interest lapsed, the evolution would stop; but while it lasted the flow of new forms could be instantaneous. Only on the earth time scale would they have to be spread out.

Obviously this is very difficult to understand. The thing to hang on to in your thought is 'sequence'. There is always sequence and apparently on the next level you can pick any sequence out of the library and take as long as you like looking at it. Even in a timeless zone nothing makes sense unless it is in consecutive order. If we look deliberately at our memories, we find that they are sequences, but not in any earth-time order. Memory, like dreaming, really belongs to the second whorl of the spiral. A sequence appears to be complete in itself and cushioned at either end by nondescript matters, so that it does not become confused with other sequences.

Since a sequence can be located on either side of 40 inches (the point of death) a sequence must endure for ever. Free will, if it exists at all, must be the manner in which your mind views a given sequence on a given whorl of the spiral. Since the spiral is always extending, so must your contemplation of a sequence extend. You may notice on another whorl things about it which never attracted your attention on earth. It also appears that after earth life, you can contemplate other people's sequences as well as your own, which must lead to a very great extension of the information available to your mind and so to mental evolution.

Talismans, Mana, Holy Men

Mankind in general is not far enough advanced mentally to be able to stand on its own feet. There has to be some link with its higher level to keep it in decency and order. This was appreciated by the Greeks long before the birth of Christ, and their ethical standard bore a close resemblance to that of Western Europe in the days of chivalry. Failure to hand on this ethic from generation to generation leads to devolution on a wide scale, as can be observed all over the world today. If the only way in which you compel the acceptance of the ethic is to say that it is God's Will, it is surely better to do this, even if the so-called proofs of it may seem somewhat improbable. All this is so obvious that it ought not to be necessary even to mention it; yet in comparatively recent times four great nations (France, Russia, Germany and China) have collapsed into periods of appalling sadistic abomination, simply through neglect of the guiding rules of human behaviour, which all knew and did not observe.

The alternative to this is the way of Victorian science, leading to a belief in no outside creator and the rule of chance. Chance appears to be absurd. Everything is far too complicated and detailed to have been evolved from living jelly without a prodding finger. How does an embryo grow into an adult without a blueprint for the developing cells to follow? How does that embryo, having followed a line of evolving development for a long way, suddenly drop off a couple of toes on each of its feet? The trouble is that you cannot use the Victorian criteria of weighing and measuring to understand the mind. Perhaps you can say that certain electric circuits will produce certain phenomena in the brain. But that brain is only an instrument of the mind and you have got no way further at all. We know that the brain does this and that without having to bother about the electric circuits. Likewise we are now finding (with pendulum or divining rod) certain things about the mind, which may in the end make it possible to reunite science and religion. Mind may be inherent in everything, from the hydrogen in space to the seagull on the mast-head. The pendulum appears to tell us that it is. If this is indeed so, then surely the mind is the same thing the church calls the 'Will of God'. We know from experiment that it can be divisible into fractions. I have talked about this in detail in other books, but must do so briefly again here.

It is very difficult for somebody, who is really only an archaeologist and anthropologist, to talk about matters on which we pay philosophers to think and pronounce. However, anthropologists have known more curious things about the minds of less civilised peoples than have ever come into the orbit of their philosophical colleagues. Isolated peoples have talked, for instance, about 'mana'; something not easily explained, but apparently some emanation from a living person added to the objects he possessed. Certain personal belongings of members of a tribe are destroyed at that person's death, for fear of the mana which is in them. We know that there is something in this belief, because we can find traces of it with the pendulum. Why should sling-stones found in an Iron Age camp, slung two thousand years ago, react to the rates of anger, war, man and thought, unless these rates had been split off from the minds of the slingers? The pendulum will tell you too, apparently, how many years ago this happened. It sounds incredible, yet it works. The pendulum dates only differ by a hundred years or so from our archaeological estimates.

Three sets of sling-stones found inside Iron Age earthworks in this area (Sidbury, Blackbury and Pilsdon Pen) all react to a date of 320 BC, which apparently indicates the time at which the Durotriges from the continent invaded the district. Yet other sling-stones from Wandlebury outside Cambridge give a date a hundred years later. Apparently our higher level mind can produce information in an instant, which our ordinary earth brain certainly could only guess at by a long process of comparison and reference to other sites.

These attempts at dating formed part of a deliberate experiment. My wife and I tried to find out whether we too could impress something of our minds on stones, which previously contained nothing of the sort. All the sling-stones from the three local camps were rounded pebbles of flint from the shingle of neighbouring beaches. The earthworks themselves are some miles inland and only man could have brought the pebbles to the hilltops. For instance Pilsdon is 900 feet above sea level and five miles inland, yet it is full of these beach pebbles, evidently slung into it in war.

Therefore for our experiment we collected a couple of hundred similar pebbles with a pair of tongs from the beach at Seaton. Not having been touched by hand, they were then brought home to Hole; picked out of the bucket, one by one, with the tongs and tested for rates with the pendulum. There was no reaction except for silica. We then chose fifty each by hand and threw them at a wall. Having been picked up with the tongs, each stone was tested with the pendulum. Every one which had been thrown by my wife reacted to her 29 inch rate for femininity and to the rate for thought. With mine each reacted to 24 inches for masculinity and also for thought. Of course there was no rate for anger as with the Iron Age stones. The experiment appeared to be most convincing. It could be repeated as long as there are pebbles on the beach and people to throw them.

There is no difficulty in devising similar experiments. In fact an ordinary letter reacts to many of the rates for the writer's characteristics, although if you test the envelope you may get mixed up with the postman.

I have no intention of spending hours demonstrating that mana exists. Everyone in antiquity knew that it did, even if they did not use the word, and it is easy to show its presence today. What it is is another matter; but it is clearly operated by the mind, whenever you do anything. Once it has been connected with an object, it apparently remains there as long as that object exists. It is the stuff that ghosts and memories are made of, and how can you weigh or measure them? It is clear that modern science is far from complete in its outlook. Some of that outlook too is not very entrancing. Think of that terrible man who cut the faces off hundreds of tiny flies to see if they would breed without them. When I first read of this, the disgust of belonging to the same species as that sage haunted me for several days. It is the same mental disease as that which caused the Inquisition. Both types of men are utterly satisfied with their own importance and have no glimmerings of real imagination at all. You cannot blame them; they are just low-grade breeds of man. If the Buddhists know anything about it, these people have a very long and dismal path ahead of them.

There can never have been many trained thinkers at any one time in ancient days, yet it is extraordinary how far they got with their thinking. Indeed it seems possible to me that the germs of their knowledge came in the first instance from outside this planet. This is not the place to discuss such apparent fantasy, but even in mediaeval books, like the *Arabian Nights*, you find the belief that each letter had a ray and the right combination was a thing of power. Look for a moment at the tale of 'Wisdom below the Severed Heads' (as translated by Mardrus and Mathers):

Now tell me to what talismans owe their virtue . . . They owe their sublime virtues and miraculous effects to the letters which compose them; for there is no letter in the language, which is not governed by a spirit, a ray, or emanation of the virtue of Allah. The spirits of the intellect communicate with those of the soul, and those of the soul with those of the senses. Letters form words and words form sentences; and the sentences written upon Talismans are nothing but a collection of spirits which, though they may astonish the ordinary man do not trouble the wise; for the wise know the power of words and are aware that words govern the whole world.

With the pendulum we can begin to see the truth at the back of this; for we are getting a rate and number for every thought form, and a letter is such a thought form. Actually a very great proportion of the trouble all over the world is caused by words, for few people read the same meaning into them as anybody else.

Ordinary everyday personal letters frequently give an impression quite different from that the writers intended them to give. The intention may be excellent; but the result can be chaos and rage. This is due to something not understood in the rays of the words themselves. The Moslems knew that this was so six hundred or more years ago.

In fact the Moslems were far in advance of the Christian peoples in the fields of learning for many hundreds of years. In mathematics, as well as in some artistic endeavours, they set fashions, which still remain a part of Western civilisation today. They seem to have grasped that what we now call parapsychology, or extrasensory perception, was an integral part of the knowledge of the wise and that it worked.

We know that large numbers of Indian holy men have for centuries, even millennia, believed in the study of extrasensory perception and that they could move from place to place instantly by changing their personal rate. The Buddhists believed the same. The Christian church, although it had saints who could fly, see visions and so on, objected to any manifestations of what they believed to be supernatural powers; although their founder spent His working life making use of them. This seems very strange when looked at objectively; but the answer may well be that the leaders of the church (like many scientists) were devoid of the potential necessary to perform the simplest exercises in ESP.

Sounds, Ultrasonic Vibrations

It is hard to study the question of the Arabs and their talisman beliefs without some genuine specimens to test. It is not difficult to make a list of rates for the letters of our alphabet. Ours goes A 12, B 13, etc; this is also the alphabet used for any Roman talisman. But where do you go from here? Probably it would be obvious to someone who habitually solves acrostics or crossword puzzles but to me it is impossible. My particular type of brain does not work in that way. It is made more difficult when I have also found the rates for notes with a pendulum and tuning fork. Here the note A is 5 and it repeats at every 10 inches. One would think therefore that on the next mental level the tonic scale is 10 instead of 8.

A in the alphabet is 12; A in music is 5. Yet there is good reason for thinking that ultrasonic vibrations affect the pendulum. I presume that the answer here is that the alphabet A has a different sound or vibration from the A in music. Yet, if you want to construct a talisman (let us call it a charm, for that is what it is) it seems to me that you probably need the sonic, as opposed to the written, alphabet. It is the mental picture of the sound which will do the work; just as it made the walls of Jericho fall down, or a column of infantry in step cause a bridge to collapse. A charm to be effective has to be spoken. It is the sound which seems to work; or rather the vibration, which causes the sound, also has a certain effect in other ways.

Many people can order flies and wasps out of a room. My wife often does it and I can sometimes do it myself. It is not conceivable that they understand the language when you shout: 'Get out!' They dislike the vibration. It is probable that a simple buzzer, too high for human ears, would rid any room of flies; although it does not work unless they are flying. Some bluebottles too are immune to it and cunning too. They sit down!

Two well-known country sounds may give us a clue to all this. One is the drumming of a snipe; the other is that of a woodpecker. In the spring these two sounds are among the most attractive that anyone can hear. The curious throbbing made by the outer tail feathers of the snipe as it dives towards the earth is something which has no parallel when one hears it above the wide, green, water meadows. It is presumed to be some form of love call and made only by the cock bird. The woodpecker makes his call against the bough of a tree, the edge of the zinc cap of a telephone pole, or some other metallic object. In about two hundred yards of woodland, I have been hearing at least three cock Greater Spotted woodpeckers drumming away for the last six weeks or so. I notice they do it with rather a sly expression on their faces and look round from time to time to see if anything is resulting from their efforts. This drumming is also supposed to be a male love call. Both kinds of drumming react strongly to the pendulum rate of 16 inches for sex. Here, then, we appear to have examples of given rates of vibration being deliberately used for what we might believe to be neither more nor less than love charms.

Of course other examples come into our minds, such as the rasping made by grasshoppers rubbing their legs against the plates of their abdomens (I hate the word 'abdomen' but it is the correct term for an insect's belly). The death watch beetle makes a sharp ticking sound, apparently as a call to its mate, and there are many others. In fact the whole wonderful effect of the dawn chorus of the birds is to this end alone.

Therefore I think that it was the sound of the words of the talisman (whose rays had to be grouped like musical chords) which gave the particular expression its power, and that you had to construct the charm backwards, though how you set about it I have no idea. It must have taken a very long time to produce even one effective talisman and then it may only have been obtained by somebody observing the effect of a particular cry on his neighbours.

It is a long period of time—at least 600 years—since the Arab intellectual in Cairo or Baghdad found a clue to all this, and still very little has been done to follow up his work. His algebra was taken up by all the world; but his remarks about rays were disregarded. Even now people are only just beginning to notice that they exist.

To try to get some light on it all, it is necessary to return to what used to be known as Nature Study and to see whether the conclusions, which we were all brought up to accept, are really true. Is man, for instance, the most highly developed of all living things? An outsider looking at this world might well doubt it. Man moves in two dimensions but birds, bats and insects live and think in three. At one time also there were reptiles (the pterodactyl family) which flew. Can man, whose visual appreciation of things is of necessity more limited than that of animals which can fly, be more advanced than say a swallow, that not only spends its life moving in three planes but also uses a sense hardly developed in man, to find its way from Africa to a particular spot in England where it was born? There is no answer to this, only a point of view. Is it more advanced to be born with these extra faculties, or to observe that you have not got them and to try to develop substitutes? From a mental point of view, the second is obviously the higher stage.

Since we have been using our mental faculties to provide us with mechanical movement in a third dimension, for which we were not apparently designed, there seems to be no reason why we should not use them also to control what we may regard as a sixth sense. Carnivorous beasts apparently use it to mesmerise their prey, and birds to attract their mates. Why should we not employ it to make helpful charms if such things exist? That such things do in fact exist seems to be demonstrated by the vibrating love calls of a variety of animals.

One goes through life with a belief that if you see something it really is as you see it. You may know that a table is nothing but a series of dots joined together by an empty space, yet you regard it as a solid object on which you can lay the breakfast. How many of us ever stop to think that to your dog or cat that table must look completely different?

I was first struck by this many years ago in Mull. I was sent out to shoot rabbits for the house, in the bracken which was ruining all the grazing of the Western Islands. I shot a rabbit bolting through a little track and went to pick it up. Beside the dead rabbit lay a woodcock, which must have been sitting on the ground as the rabbit ran past. I looked at the bird in some surprise, for I had never heard of such a thing happening before. Then I realised that the eyes were set in the head in such a position that it could never see straight in front of it and must have two pictures in its mind at once. How did it sort them out?

It has occurred to me since then that the zigzag flight of such birds as snipe or dunlin is because they wish to fly on a given line and cannot see directly along this line of flight. The axis of the zigzags would be the course they wished to take, swinging out to either side so that each eye in turn could look along it.

Of course birds are not alone in being unable to see straight ahead. A hare cannot do so. I have watched one running towards me across a twenty-acres field in Cambridgeshire. It came straight on, ran over my foot and apparently never saw me at all.

As I said previously some cats cannot distinguish objects unless they are moving. People often think that their cats are blind, because they cannot recognise stationary objects. Even if they were it would hardly matter, for their radar through their whiskers is so good.

The fact appears to be that no living animal ever sees anything as it really is. All that happens is that a series of vibrations produces a certain result in that animal's brain. By convention we learn to call the effects of these vibrations sights, sounds, tastes or whatever they happen to seem to indicate. Extrasensory perception is just another of these appreciations of vibrations; but it appears to have a far wider range than any of the others and it depends on your own particular potential how much of the band of vibrations you can appreciate. Just too as you can produce mechanical sounds, or pictures and so forth, which can be appreciated by your fellows, so it is possible to make use of ESP for purposes which they can understand. For centuries this has been called magic. Whether it be the aboriginal witch doctor with his pointing bone killing his enemy by black magic, or the white conjurer distributing slips from the Bible to promote health in a Welsh hill valley, they are making use of a mental power, which science as a whole (confined to the five obvious senses) has not attempted to understand.

How does the local white witch remove warts for instance? All countrymen know, or used to know, that this can be done. I got a wart on my hand at the end of the last war and went one day into a smart and up-to-date chemist in Oban. Behind the counter was a tidy, modern, young man in a clean white overall. I asked him for a caustic pencil to remove the wart. He looked at me very seriously and said, 'Hadn't you better take it to the wise woman?' I was too busy to look for wise women and the caustic pencil worked, but I hardly expected to hear such a remark in a shop like that.

These conjurers still exist in this part of the world; but are viewed with contempt by those who either believe that they are witches and so (according to the Old Testament) should be killed; or, when viewed by science, are simply primitive faith healers and so not worthy of intelligent observation. Still they quietly continue to remove warts, or cure ring worm, often with great effect. They are using a higher-level force to cure an earth-level complaint and this is a 'miracle'. Of course they must not be paid in money for apparently there is not any on the second level; but you may give them a chicken or something of that kind.

We divide our subjects into groups and are inclined to specialise in one watertight compartment. Archaeology, history, folk lore and medicine are really all interlinked and all part of the study of man. You cannot study man either, without taking in geology, botany and zoology as well. But today less and less is being taught in ever greater detail by more and more people. There is no wide-ranging school which could give degrees in general knowledge and thus ensure that a body of men existed who were really educated.

The point I am trying to make is that ESP is not a watertight subject and it will be found to overlap many others. If you have two or more mental levels, naturally ESP will provide links with all subjects on the higher levels. It is simply a question of having something which will bridge the gap between the levels of vibration. The thought, which produces the vibrations, is

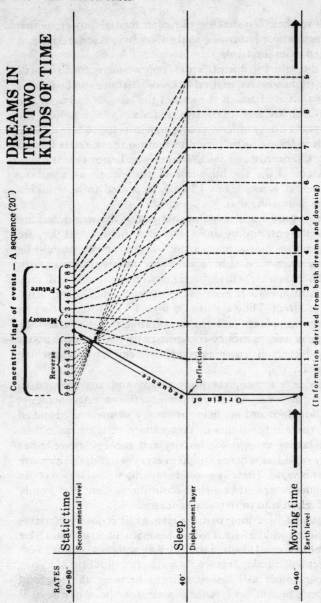

Figure 5 Although many people have a dislike for diagrams, I hope they will give this one some attention. It attempts to show why events may be appreciated in dreams, either in reversed order, or before they have taken place in earth time. There would be no spaces between the numbers on the top line.

vibrating on both; but, as far as I can work it out, those on the higher level are four times as fast as those in our earth mind.

In sleep your mind appears to go right out through the second level and has no recollection of what happens when it returns; but during its passage on to a still higher grade, it passes through the second zone and there it picks up its dreams, which are memories. These, as we have said already, can be past or future and may belong to you or somebody else. They are real memories and not imagination. One morning as I was waking I thought I saw a bottle of Gordon's gin standing by itself on the bedside table. In reality the table was heaped high with books. When I went to bed that night I noticed that on a second table, which was now beside the bed and otherwise bare of objects, there was a copy of a magazine lying face downwards. The whole of the back cover was an advertisement in colour for Gordon's gin and in one corner of it was a large picture of a bottle of gin standing upright. One would think that it was such a trivial incident that it must be a coincidence. But it is not. It happens with great frequency. Let us look at a diagram for a moment (Figure 5).

The two horizontal lines represent two successive mental levels with the earth plane at the bottom. On this line some events in a sequence are represented by numbered divisions as on a ruler. They are separated since they are moving in time. On the higher horizontal line, the same sequence should be represented as a minute dot, but, entirely for convenience, we will separate and number each event in the same order as on the line below. There appears to be no moving time here; the events should be complete spheres surrounding the dot and without thickness or distance separating them. We cannot represent them in this way. We will be content with an expanded section of the sequence in a single plane. You find at once that on this second level, you have two marks for each event instead of the single one on the line below. The sequence can proceed backwards as well as forwards. Owing to the fact that the sequence has a rate on the Spiral of Rates, the second timeless origin of it will not be directly above the point of origin below. If your spiral coils outwards in a clockwise manner, the upper point of origin will be further out than the lower one. In a horizontal plane it will be about 80 inches, or two metres, higher up.

The events on the upper line are memories. If we now join the corresponding numbered points on the two lines, we find three possible kinds of memory; past, future and reversed; which type they will be depends on how far you have moved along the lower line. On the diagram the change from past to future memory occurs at 40. In any case you can only obtain a future memory when your mind has moved in sleep, or death, up to the higher level. That appears to be the explanation of all mediumistic foresight and of future dreams.

One other factor comes out of this. Owing to the expansion of the spiral, the points of origin of a given sequence on two levels can never be exactly above one another. Therefore the memory picture can never, in the parlance of colour painting, register exactly. A prophecy will never be completely right; although much of it may be, a remembered incident will always have some errors, however slight, in it.

I know this is very hard to understand and even more difficult to put into words. It took me hours of work to produce a diagram which gave me even moderate satisfaction; although I have been constructing diagrams for years. It is one thing to have to produce a diagram showing a section through a Dark Ages earthwork and what you have found in it, and quite another to have to deal with one explaining what appears to happen between two levels of the mind. However, both are based on observed fact as far as I am concerned. I knew exactly where a particular scrap of pottery should be placed on a given plan and I know exactly how a given thought form fits into a particular picture.

8 Dreams, Breeding and Heredity

It is known from long years of scientific experiment that nothing is really like our senses tell us. The apparently solid hall table, which we can see, touch, measure and even at times, smell or hear if it creaks, is not only a series of infinitesimal particles joined together by great areas of empty space; but it is the brain's interpretation of a series of thought forms in code. A certain series of rays from the minute particles gives us the mental interpretation of a solid table. However, it is clear that by frequently changing the rate of vibrations of the rays of which it is composed, you could have hundreds of differing tables in the same space; but they would be invisible to us on our present level of existence. In sleep a different one would be appreciable. It would not be the one on which we dump our letters for the post, although it might look so alike you could not tell the difference. But, owing to the spiral, the hall tables would not be one on top of the other in the same volume of space but they would for each mental level be both further from the centre of the earth and also to one side of a vertical line.

This applies too to the observer. When he goes to sleep, his earth body remains where it was; in bed perhaps. But his mental self, his spirit, soul or whatever you like to call it, moves up on to another level from which, if he remains alive, it can return; but, if he dies in his sleep, it does not come back. In each case the rate on which this takes place is 40 inches on the pendulum.

So far it is all reasonably clear, as was noted earlier in the book. At 40 inches you rise into the second level and at 80 inches you presumably enter the third; although in this case the pendulum says that there is no curtain of sleep, or death, to pass. There is a mass of corroborative evidence pointing out that this theory is probably true. Large numbers of people have reported that when in a high fever, wounded, under an anaesthetic and so on, or even simply overtired, they have apparently woken up and found themselves looking down on their own bodies from a position to one side. In every case I have read, or had sent to me in a letter, or been told by word of mouth, the second position was between 6½ and 7 feet above the resting body. This is exactly what the pendulum says. It is then the third zone and not the one crowded with memory dots

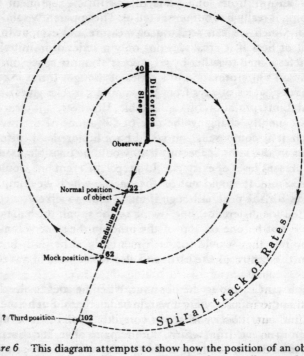

Figure 6   This diagram attempts to show how the position of an object appears to change in relation to the observer as he mentally ascends the Spiral of Rates. The object chosen was a silver spoon with a rate of 22 inches. On the second whorl it appears 62 instead of 22 inches distant. This shows why persons reporting 'out of the body' experiences say that they look down on themselves.

(the second) which is a new life. Only in a flash between two and three will you be able to see your earth body again, once you have left the zone of memories. It is coming back from sleep, or passing into it, that you make contact accidentally with some memories and then dream (Figure 6).

If I have thought this out right, the so-called Heaven of religious beliefs is another zone of living less than the height of an ordinary room above our heads, or perhaps twice as high. We cannot see it because all its vibrations, whether of light, sound, colour, or any other kind, are too fast to register in our earth brains. Since the construction of earthly objects is in reality almost empty space, there is no difficulty for parts of one zone to pass invisibly through the other; although apparently everything on the third level will seem as real and solid to people living on that level as things do on this earth level. Earth then appears to consist of concentric zones of living all quite close together. Presumably you could destroy the whole present earth's skin with everything on it without making any difference to the one above, unless it was shocked surprise at such a stupid action.

Whether these zones, or onion skins, go on out into space to infinity there is no means of telling without using a pendulum of too great length to be convenient; but there is certainly a fourth above the third. The probability is that mind is indestructible, time limitless and the skins innumerable.

This is such an important matter that I do not for a moment expect anyone to believe what I have written in this chapter, without making rigorous tests themselves. Perhaps a third of the population cannot do so; but at least another third could do it easily and with very little trouble. It is also entirely personal. If you want to know whether you are extinguished at death, or continue to infinity you can find out. I have told you how you can find out, if I have reasoned correctly from observed facts. There is no need to swallow the theories of either church or science. You can obtain your own information and reason from it yourself. I am not responsible for your conclusions. It is up to you to find the answer for yourself. You have to be the judge of the probabilities of your own future. Of course you always were, although faith in someone else's theories was often considered to be necessary. But how reliable were the theories of the theologians of AD 400, or of scientists before the splitting of the atom? Everything has changed with very great rapidity and those who can be bothered to think, must think again.

Actually it is quite devastating to realise how few people ever think at all. They mostly take their ideas from what they are told on the wireless, television, or in the newspapers, from people who are prepared to take a reasonable fee. To suggest anything different makes you tread on many corns of vested interest. No professional pathfinder likes you for doing it.

I have written frequently that I am always ready to change any of my ideas should they be shown to be wrong. Occasionally I have had to do so and said it in a succeeding book. It is much the same when working the pendulum. Since one of the components which make it work is mental, the operator must view his results with complete detachment. There must be no hoping that the answer will be this or that. Strong concentration on that answer may very well produce a completely faulty one.

The reason why this should happen seems to be that we are dealing with two distinct mental units; although both of them are probably our own and one is not that of some stranger on a higher level. The higher-level mind vibrates much faster than the lower and is in a sense more tenuous. Therefore if you concentrate too much on the lower mind, the higher one is swamped and the lower one produces the answer. In innumerable cases we find that the higher unit knows very much more than the lower one could possibly know, but in others the answer may well be our earth-level guess.

Naturally I am very uncertain about this and feel there is probably a succession of units and one does not know with which one the pendulum makes its contact. The solution should be answered, however, by the numbering of the rates and each level presumably has its range of 40 inches. Thus if you set the pendulum at 22 for silver, you contact silver, which you can see, touch and so on for it is earth silver. However, if you set the pendulum at 62 and contact silver, you may find nothing visible if you go to look for it. It is there all right but it is in the next mental plane. Of course it can be in both, yet it need not be so. It may be simply a memory of silver on the second level.

I know this all sounds very difficult and possibly absurd. No one may believe that there are many separate levels of mind and that our earth mind is the lowest that we know about. Presumably the 'subconscious' is lower still and is only animal and to treat it as of vital importance instead of trying to smother it is a very great mistake. All advance in culture appears to be based on the very repressions which psychologists attempt to remove. There can be no civilisation without discipline to order the relationship of one man towards another. If you remove the so-called complexes, on which psychologists thrive, you destroy discipline and civilisation goes with it. For you cannot train a child to rational behaviour towards its fellows without restrictions. Remove the restrictions and you get an animal. Not only that, unless you can appreciate that your protection by your fellows in bulk can only be bought by a certain duty to help and protect them, you are living in a world in which a carnivorous monster may at any time jump over the hedge and bite out your throat. The friendly exchange of duty between the members of a community keeps the monster in check.

Another difficulty is that there must be a personal code number and at present there is no clue as to how to find it. How widely would it differ from that of your next-door neighbour or an Australian aborigine? The whole question of heredity is an unsolved problem. You can breed a wild horse from the Steppes so that in time it acquires the extreme elegance and beauty of a Derby winner. But then you can reverse the process and in turn make its offspring revert to the scraggy objects named after Prevalski. All dogs and wolves apparently can breed together and produce fertile offspring and yet what could be apparently more different than a Great Dane and a Dachshund? What effect, if any, has selective breeding through the ages had on the mentality of man? Are all men blood relations or not? And this question is now becoming more complicated when people are asking whether humanity at one time had an infusion of foreign blood from another planet. If it did, of course all men are not brothers in anything but a remote sense. As men pry into the past, more and more evidence begins to collect in favour of this theory, which would have seemed quite fantastic at the beginning of the century. Although very much a child of the Edwardian period, and regarding that lost age as infinitely more civilised than the present, I do not view this strange idea as absurd. Neither do the canny scientists of Soviet Russia, who of all people appear to set the least store on heredity.

The reason why heredity comes into this story is a curious one. Some years ago when I had been working on the old gods of Britain, I published the results in a book (somewhat misguidedly called *Witches*, which was not really its subject). Among the pen friends which this book produced, were representatives of the old Witch religion. There are still some of these, who are quite distinct from the modern imitative covens. As far as I have learnt, the witch religion hardly differed from that of the gypsies before they became Christian. It was a relatively simple nature creed, but it made very great use of the psi factor. It generated power by mass excitement and anchored it in stones or trees. I have not been told how it was taken out again; but many people must have heard how the Hampshire witches sent a 'Cone of Power' against the Armada and in theory caused the storm which ruined the enterprise.

Now we come to the key point of this apparent digression. The witches (and probably the gypsies too) were in the habit of deliberately breeding people to increase their psychic powers. This is presumably why so many gypsies tell fortunes to this day. It is not their particular race or land of distant origin which gives them this faculty. It is simply our old friend selective breeding. Also, since this is obviously something which was tested by generations of trial and error, we must assume that the psi faculty can be bred in the human mind. It is not something mystic and wonderful outside it; but is just one of our senses, which science has neglected to study.

Of course this takes some of the gilt off the gingerbread. The semi-religious awe with which the prophecies of the wise woman were hailed receives something of a cold douche when one realises that she is really only using one of the faculties with which every human being should be provided. Of course some are born without it, but then there are many people who cannot tell red from green. Since most of us can tell this, it is hard for us to appreciate what those other unfortunates must see and it is equally hard to explain to them the beauty of a sunset over the Western Ocean. If we could not see this, would we not be ready to make use of any aid to understand what it was really like? Why then all this irritable and often absurd denial of the existence of a faculty which most people do possess in some degree? I'm afraid the answer is that it is a kind of religious dogma going back to the legendary Witch of Endor in the Bible. Today such an outlook is ridiculous. Many things take place which are far less natural than being able to jump in mind from one level of existence to another. It is much odder really, to be able to fly, or to swim beneath the ocean in a submarine than to be able to see what is happening on another mental level. We were evidently designed to do this, but the other two accomplishments are artificially acquired. If it is natural to breed horses with the enhanced speed of a Derby winner, it is also natural to breed people who can foresee the future. In either case whether it is a matter of great importance depends on your outlook. It takes a long time and much trouble to achieve the desired result and we cannot expect modern witches to burst out into full-blooded mediums after a few convocations.

The important thing in all this is that the energy, which supplies the psychic phenomena, if we like to call them that, is developed on our own earth level and is not some strange supernatural current, or anything like that. In fact, as I have tried to stress before, there is no such thing as supernatural, except in so far as the word can be applied to whatever force or personality set the whole Universe in being. It may be, as some think, that that force is 'Nature', or as others prefer to speak of it, 'God'; but that is the only force which can possibly be supernatural.

People write to me and say they know there is a supernatural, because they have seen a ghost of a close relative. But those are not supernatural. They are no more or less supernatural than the pictures on their television screen. They are simply thought images outside their normal time and space. You do not see the people on the television screen as they appear to be in your room. It is not taking place in your vicinity at all. It is the same with the ghost of your uncle. It is a picture someone has photographed as it were on to an electronic field, which you have been on the right wavelength to contact. Most ghosts are of this nature and not at all unlike the pictures we see of people in dreams.

9 Telepathy

Nobody ever mentioned telepathy to me until I was twenty-three. Then to my great surprise, for I had been reading serious biology and zoology at Cambridge for some years, an old and apparently very down to earth colonel started to discuss the subject at a dinner party. If you have never heard of such a faculty, you are incredulous at first. However, no one could doubt the colonel. He had just been talking about the Solingen blades of some Arab swords and how they closely resembled those of the crusaders. I knew something about that and even that a Solingen blade had a crescent moon engraved on it. If the old man could talk so much sense on one rather uncommon subject, presumably there was sense in what he said about this other strange phenomenon.

My besetting sin is curiosity. Having heard of telepathy I had to find out more about it. It was soon evident that the learned men of Cambridge, and indeed my friends outside the place, were divided into three classes: (1) Those who had not the slightest interest in telepathy. (2) Those who forcefully denied that such a faculty could exist. (3) Those who knew that it did exist from personal experience and viewed the doubters with contempt. In my own case I found that I had simply failed to observe the phenomenon. It often happened, but since I did not know that there was such a thing, I had taken its occurrence in every case to be coincidence.

There is an absurd idea that men are all more or less alike. A drug which suits one patient is supposed to suit all others; whereas it frequently has disastrous effects on some of them. Every man differs from every other, thus falsifying statistics and making nonsense of computers. Some men react to telepathy and take it as a matter of course. Others do not and are firmly convinced that there is no such thing. It is another of these inadequacies, like those we observed over the operation of the pendulum and compared with colour blindness. I think telepathy is the most widespread of all the manifestations of psi activity, and few are those who never experience it.

There are other strange matters to which attention never seems to be drawn. I had a man helping me at an excavation of a Christian Saxon cemetery at Burwell, Cambridgeshire. He was down in a grave scraping small particles of soil into a biscuit tin for removal. It made a small tinkling sound. I went over to see how he was getting on. He looked up and said how much he was enjoying it as it made such a pretty colour. I knew that I had always thought he was a bit odd and now he seemed quite mad. However, I decided to ask what sort of colour it made. He told me it was a lovely pale pink. I went on talking about it and found that he appreciated all sounds in colour and thought everybody else did too. It amazed him that I had never seen a coloured sound. Of course I may be the unusual one. I rather concentrate on colour in my mind. If I am doing watercolour sketches, I always memorise the colours, making a pencil sketch, then taking it and the colours back indoors before doing any painting. So you have no difficulty with constantly-changing light and shade.

I have since met an occasional person who admitted that he sensed sounds in colour, but not very many. Far more people put colour labels on to smells. I can do this to a limited extent; but with me it is only a trick of associated idea. Others, I think, really notice a 'dark green smell' or something of the kind.

It is with wild life that telepathy really comes into its own. Anybody can observe this, even in suburban surroundings. Just watch the turning and twisting of a flock of starlings, or two blue tits chasing in and out of bushes. Two birds or a hundred turn as one, because the thought passes instantaneously between all their minds. No call is necessary. The leading bird just thinks what he is going to do. Telepathy does the rest. Whether telepathy is conveyed by ultrasonic sound I very much doubt, for sound is relatively slow as you can see if you watch a man hammering in a post on the opposite side of a valley.

Different species can talk to one another by telepathy. I have frequently thought a cat into coming to me from a hundred yards away. I have watched cats obviously talking to foxes and I have felt a fox looking at me so that I turned round expecting to see a human. If you have a great friend of the same species as yourself the link becomes so strong that you are always getting the same idea at the same instant and it is often difficult to tell in whose mind it originated. You can establish very close telepathic links with animal friends too and understand their wishes without words.

A great deal has been written on this subject and I have read very little of it. With all these unknowns the point to be aimed at seems to me to be to try to determine the general shape of the problem rather than to go into narrow detail. For instance does telepathy differ very greatly from ordinary radio? Of course radio appears to you as sound, but if you receive a telepathic message you understand it in words. You decode it in some way. You could not possibly receive a message in words from a cat or a dog; but to your mind the message arrives as 'I want my supper please', or something like that. When you hear a thing on the radio, you are not hearing the actual words spoken in a London studio but something which has been broken down into code from the original words, projected, received miles away and decoded into words once more. This seems to be very similar to telepathy, although you decode the message into your own words and not into what the projector may have been thinking. Only the general sense comes through to your mind and this would be the same if you got a telepathic message from someone using a foreign language, which you did not understand. You would decode it automatically into your native speech.

It seems to be clear that telepathy is a far more diffused method of communication than is the word of mouth. Of course it is not so exact as we know it, but who can talk in English to a dog which has been trained to Gaelic orders? It looks very much as if its use could be greatly expanded by training and practice; although it might be necessary to start this training in early childhood.

Undoubtedly there is evidence that some dreams are passed between individuals by telepathy. The case of Mrs Beresford and the stray budgerigar is an example. A few days ago I had one reported by my wife, which directly concerns this book. If the reader turns back to the beginning he will find a rather trivial attempt. to guess what a dilemma might have been expected to look like to people long ago, and that in American terms it would have had a 'mean' expression. When I wrote this I was thinking of something like a fierce and dangerous little bull. My wife had not read this notebook then. On this particular day she woke from a dream. She had had a worrying time involving her mother and some Americans. They had been mixed up with a fierce little black bull. When she told me this I gave her the manuscript to look at. I had been reading it over the night before and it was beside my bed. I had not mentioned it and had not talked about it at all. She had no idea what I was writing about. This is a sample of some kind of telepathy. In her sleep my wife had taken thought forms from my sleeping mind. But all this is beyond the pendulum notation for sleep and death. It is beyond our ordinary earth progress. So I think (never believing that I know anything except about the Dark Ages and how to handle a sailing-ship or a body of men) that we are really in two worlds at once and that telepathy belongs to the higher one.

Looked at dispassionately it seems to mean that we live in two worlds and can slip from one to the other without much trouble. Apparently the second one is higher than the 40 inch rate for death. Laugh this off if you can. It seems to mean that death is only a curtain between two levels of living. How can you avoid this conclusion from what we have already found out?

I am not trying to push any particular belief. I just cannot see how the evidence can lead to any other conclusion. Materialists, rationalists and all the rest of them may believe that they know the answer, but they had not that information available to children, who found pennies in the ditch with a cotton reel tied on a length of thread. In fact they were too clever by half and could not see the wood for the trees. Jesus said: 'Except ye be converted and become as little children, ye shall not enter the Kingdom of Heaven.'

It is a mistake to interpret this exactly, for surely it only means that, unless you grow up realising that there are at least two mental levels, it will be very hard to appreciate this fact later. Thanks to the various devices of television, children today grow up in a world in which it would not surprise them if they slipped into the days of Julius Caesar or the building of the Great Pyramid; while the germ of the idea even entered my head as a child with Kipling's Puck stories. But if you are brought up in a setting of rigid materialism with no flashes of imagination and the greed for personal advancement as your one star, there is no chance whatever of getting beyond earthly weights and measures.

There will be no Kingdom of Heaven for such people until something completely re-fashions their mentality. Grey fact will just succeed grey fact, until they die, and even then they will find that their library of memories has nothing in it but grey facts again. There will be no gleam of sunlight on the sails of the four-masted barque coming up over the rim of the Western Ocean on the horns of the morning and bringing thoughts of Patagonia, or the Antarctic ice.

10   Future Memories

Our brief look at telepathy seems to make two points clear. One is that telepathy is a perfectly normal function of earth life, common alike to both animals and men. The second is that it does not appear to work like any of the known senses and apparently really is on a higher level. You do not use any form of human speech to talk in mind to a friend or, if it comes to that, to an animal. There is no need to bother about the opinions of those who say there is no such thing. It is perfectly obvious that there is. It is very hard to produce proof that anybody really sees or hears anything. Yet it would be absurd to deny that they do. It is the same with telepathy. Most people experience it and often with considerable frequency. Therefore we have to take it as something which exists and needs, in the cause of science, to be investigated. Have we the slightest idea what happens?

The point really is that nobody has the slightest idea how the mind (as opposed to the brain) works. Is it an individual affair, or is it something which is linked to all creation? Philosopher, prelate or layman, nobody knows the answer. Last of all seems to come the philosopher, who has been sold on the idea that the mind is the same as the brain.

We get to a point in our thinking where it is beginning to be clear that telepathy is really a function of a higher level of the mind and only by chance occurs to humans on this level at all. But this also shows that animals have minds, which are not confined to one earthly level. They are operating on two levels and apparently more efficiently than mankind. Your dog does not vanish at death any more than you do. What will happen to my wife, who has had a long succession of dearly loved cats, I don't know; but I expect quite a lot of jealous scratching and spitting. For there is no reason to assume that mentality will automatically be different on successive levels. It looks as if the exercise of living is really an attempt to train the individual mind for the purpose of moving on up the ladder. If that is so the nirvana theory of later absorption in a greater mind does not appear to be likely. The individual hives off from the mass. As he goes through time and space he apparently throws off portions of his mind into all that he handles to any considerable extent and there they remain indefinitely. So that although the individual mind is always in a state of change, it is always the one mind.

There is a great deal of evidence in support of the idea that future thoughts cast a shadow ahead of them. There was the horrible feeling at Ladram Bay, which I have described in *Ghost and Divining Rod*. Here there seems little doubt that the anguished feelings of a man about to drown himself were felt by several people years before the actual event. A very similar suicide story was recorded by a former Abbot of Downside, who blamed himself for not being able to prevent it.

However, it is not these dramatic happenings which are likely to be valuable as proof. What one needs is a simple series of repeatable experiments. Or you can get a really trivial future memory, which may be the target perhaps to aim at. Look at this: one summer day I woke up early, dreaming that I was looking out from my bed through the open casement windows on to the sunlit beech and ash trees on the hillside. In my dream a very large hornet, gleaming orange in the sunshine came in over the windowsill with a hum and vanished behind my wife's dressing table looking-glass. That was the end of the dream. It was quite dark at the time in reality and the curtains were pulled across the open window.

I fell asleep in a moment and was woken eventually by the clamour of several carrion crows disputing outside the window. As I sat up a wasp buzzed around the side of the curtain. I told it to go out and it did. When I got up later, I found an exhausted bee sitting on the dressing table where the dream hornet had vanished. It was not a fine, sunny morning but grey and overcast. You can dismiss the whole thing as coincidence, of course, but to me it is quite clear that the dream was built up out of two trivial memories of incidents which had not yet happened.

Now this kind of dream is so comparatively unimportant that, unless you are looking for such things, you would never notice it at all. However, they happen all the time. I remember somebody telling me that she had a dream about a rabbit laying eggs; got up and saw a rabbit on the lawn; went downstairs to find that the cook had run out of eggs for breakfast. There are hundreds of dreams of this kind for every one dream containing something dramatic to be found (perhaps days later) in a newspaper.

It is impossible to get away from the fact that future memories exist in the sleeping state. They must also be memories of events on earth and not on the next level. You can collect them by the hundred and anyone who denies it is simply quibbling. I have tried to explain already how I think this can be so, but whatever the explanation may be, you are still left with the uncomfortable fact that the future exists, just as the past exists. You can whistle for your dogma of free will. There doesn't appear to be any. This only holds good as far as the actual events are concerned. Where you have free will is in your mental reaction to those events. The exercise is for the mind and not the body. But who or what plans the events? You will not easily persuade me that they happen by chance. Just as our hypothetical scientist a few pages back is only a collection of small dots joined together by French knitting, so our lives seem to be in fact a series of non-existent happenings. Everything is really in the mind. Another part of you looks at a series of events in the same way that we seem to look at a television picture; although that is one more step more remote from reality. I am sorry if this is very difficult to grasp, but I must be serious sometimes; although I have realised long ago that life is not so serious as many people believe it to be. I think it may be in reality an extremely well organised film from which it is hoped by the producer that you will extract some benefit. Why he should want to do this, I cannot guess; but what else has he got to do? It would be as boring for him as for anyone else if people did not try to evolve their minds.

In the prophecies of the Brahan Seer, who came from the Outer Hebrides and was murdered on the mainland, is a series of horrific anticipations resembling those of the Day of Judgment in the Bible. But, when these are over, the exiles will return from islands as yet undiscovered in the seer's day (the seventeenth century) and re-colonise the lands of their fathers. The seer lived long before the Evictions. He did not know of New Zealand. Where did this information come from? This is not the same as the future dreams, which are something connected with our own mentality. It is foretelling unguessable things centuries before they happen.

The Brahan Seer mesmerised himself with a shining stone and clearly his mind went up on to the next mental level. But what did he find there which gave him these future glimpses? Some of his prophecies have come true already. It is no use to deny it or explain it as coincidence. These things are natural phenomena and there must be a natural answer.

I have suggested a comparison between life and a cinema film, which can be looked at both before and behind a given point. Only at the point of observation is the viewer really living. These prophecies suggest a film on a far grander scale. I am convinced that the Brahan Seer and other prophets have been able to see snippets of this larger film when their minds were running on another level, and that scraps of these snippets remained when they came back and woke up to earth life again.

Prophecies would not always be correct because their viewpoint shifted with the outward swing of the ascending spiral. A film intended to be seen directly on the earth plane would be viewed at a distorting angle from the next one. So the prophet does not often get everything right and he may misunderstand what he sees when viewed differently. The point is that the film seems to be there already and it has probably been made ready for a mass of experiments and training to be based on it.

11   Heredity

There are many other lines, which I have not attempted to follow in this study; but those which I have touched on all appear to be heading in the same direction. Nowhere in it have we seen the faintest suggestion that anything might be due to evolution by chance.

The orders of nature known as the Invertebrates seem even more convincing than any birds, or mammals. Just look at a crab, for instance, when you are getting it ready for eating. Can anybody really believe that all those complicated armoured joints reached their present shapes by each successive ancestral crab type adding something more efficient to the general family of crabs? Where did all those bristles on its legs come from? And how did it learn to extract calcium carbonate from the water to provide it with protection. As it grows bigger, it has to cast off that relatively impenetrable covering and hide naked under a rock until it can draw more calcium carbonate to it to form a new shell. Presumably this elaborate process feels like death and a new birth to a crab, but how did it learn to do it? Actually there are very early fossil crabs in the geological record and they are obviously crabs already. It would appear that there must have been blueprints for each type of crab; or how else could the cells of which they are composed possibly have developed. If you gave each cell the wisdom of Solomon, it could not have thought out what to do. Some other entity must have thought up the plans and drawn the blueprints.

Look at our British butterflies and you will see that there is a basic pattern of ornamentation beneath the colouration of very many of them. Fritillaries, Tortoiseshells, Painted Ladies and so on appear to be variations of one theme, with which someone could have been experimenting. The three bars on the top side of the upper wing of many, for instance, are constant in this design. Or the eyes on the lower wing of some, which vary in number, must have been deliberately put there to frighten off potential enemies. Explain to me, if you can, how such things developed on the wings of butterflies by trial and error. For example how did the tiny scales on the wings arrange themselves in the form of eyes at all?

The whole of this subject is simply a mass of unsolved questions and when this happens it is a sure sign that there is something wrong with the original theories. What decides that, at a given stage of development, the eye of a flat fish should travel right over its head and fix itself beside its opposite eye? Of course the answer to why it has to move is that it will not be irritated by the sand on the bottom on which it will spend the rest of its life. But we are told that acquired characteristics cannot be transmitted to the offspring. This is an acquired characteristic, yet the changeover happens with every flat fish. The next answer is that it must be a gene. Who put in the gene? How many soles were blind in one eye before something told a gene what to do? How was the eye moved little by little in each successive generation of fish? It must have taken untold generations before the eye became clear of the sand. But if someone directed the change from outside, there is no difficulty at all. Furthermore, as there is apparently no moving time on the next level, the eons necessary for the change would pass in a flash. A theory of deliberate planning makes sense. The theory of chance evolution does not, neither does it work. Much that it calls evolution is not evolution at all, but devolution. Genes may give the orders to the growing cells in a body but somebody must have given those orders to the genes. Each one is like a given button on a switchboard. Someone has to press the button. So here is a whole great subject in which it seems imperative to infer the hand of an external planner.

Here is a wasp crawling on my paper. Who taught it to make a paper nest by chewing up wood, to make wax cells for its children and to fill those cells with honey for the children to eat. Just explain how this complicated arrangement could have evolved by chance improvements, however many million years it took in the process.

There is also the little solitary wasp, who took possession of the lock in the kitchen cupboard. Who taught it to hunt a particular kind of spider; paralyse this by a sting in exactly the right place; take it in at the keyhole and leave it with an egg on it beside other spiders of the same species. Then it cemented up the keyhole till it was almost invisible. In time the eggs hatched out and the grubs found exactly the right quantity of living meat for them to eat.

Is there anything to suggest that someone did not organise it all? The descent of man from monkeys has been discarded for years. Attempts are now made to suggest that man evolved from some unknown ancestor like a lemur. Is there any reason why he should have done so? Why should he not have been dumped here fully developed? I was brought up as a Darwinist and it took me more than a generation to begin to doubt the original theory. Once doubt creeps in everything blows away like thistle-down. There is nothing solid behind it. Evolution remains obvious, but it looks far more like deliberate planning. Chance drops out. The belief in chance is simply a form of religious dogma.

It is hard to see why all this should have become so rigid. The trouble over finding a missing link between men and monkeys should surely have made people wonder whether any of the rest of it was correct. Why were they so set on not having it all planned by a superior mentality? Other men in all ages had believed this to be the correct answer. Why did the Victorians jump at any theory, however shaky, which suggested otherwise? The only possible answer that I can think of is that they were so pleased with themselves that they could not abide the idea of any mind being superior to their own. This conceit is rather pathetic in a species which obviously cannot manage its own affairs.

We have pried into many strange and dark corners in this chase of the dilemma. It may still be lurking in one of them, with horrid red eyes glowing in the dusk. However, I think we have made it shrink and worn its horns to stumps.

I think the worst wound it got came from a completely

unexpected quarter. Who could have guessed that a simple pendulum would reveal a vast catalogue of identifying numbers? If anything points to external planning, this must surely do so. Every thought form which flits through our minds is classified by two and probably many more co-ordinates. Our minds did not make them up; they are there for us to find and wonder at. These numbers can be found by other methods quite distinct from any form of divination and they are not particular to any one individual. They must be in some external entity's catalogue, which we happen to have found. There is no reason to suppose that they were put there for our convenience, rather the reverse. We may not have been meant to know about them at all, but, having found them, we now know much more about the behaviour of birds, beasts and insects. They have a built-in radar and, in the case of insects, this has also been identified by elaborate electronic apparatus. It appears to make nonsense of the idea of insects navigating by the stars, which is currently fashionable. Blame P. Callagan in America, who has found it by highly respectable, scientific means and not by my simple magic. But, if you can do it with a champagne cork on a length of thread, why bother to spend hundreds of pounds on electronic equipment?

Much more comes out of the pendulum study than that. It shows that time as we know it does not appear to exist on a higher mental level to which our minds apparently go when we are asleep and on which they appear to stay more or less permanently when we die. I think not permanently because there apparently are higher levels above that one, on which moving time seems to return again.

How would Darwin's ape be capable of dealing with these problems? Obviously not at all; it is hard enough to train one to ride a tricycle. How do the philosophers get round it? They quibble and say that all mentality resides in the brain and that (since the brain decays after death) nothing remains. This seems to be nonsense, for we know, as we have seen already, that something detached from a mind remains for an indefinite period in the things which that particular person has used. Of course the bulk of the mind must persist too. In fact mind must be immortal.

Then heredity comes into the puzzle. We can see that the resulting personality is built up from factors derived from many different ancestors. We are told that it is in the genes, but even if it is, somebody seems to have played about with these genes until he built up the particular personality. Why should this be? I think the answer could be that he wanted to test the personality against a given set of conditions and see how it reacted to them. The conditions were already fixed. Only the mentality of the individual could appreciate and think about them.

It would be interesting to know how much say heredity has in the composition of a people, or an individual. Has it any say in anything except the bodily construction? Did not Napoleon say: 'The English are the finest infantry in the world. Fortunately there are not many of them'? By English, of course, he meant great, raw-boned Jocks from the Highlands as much as placid ploughmen from Suffolk. It is a very great compliment and it is worth remembering it when you see these willy wet-winkles thronging the streets. They too could be polished up and turned into fighting men. Before the Second World War I frequently heard men, who had survived the earlier one, remarking that the boys coming on were no good and would not fight if it came to trouble. I always opposed the view, saying that it was in the blood and that they would be as good as their fathers.

I have implied that both mind and body are influenced by heredity and yet I am not sure that this is right. Obviously the environmental influence can be completely negative. You could take five hundred children and bring them up in an art school and, unless they were born with the vital spark, no single one would grow up to be an artist.

This seems to be one of those cases where one has to be one's own guinea-pig. What do I know about myself, which might throw some light on it? My father died when I was eight. He was a good watercolour artist, painting insects and tiny landscapes. Although he had been a regular soldier he was extremely interested in archaeology, botany and zoology. I never saw much of his work and I was sixteen when I started to take an interest in drawing. I began with insects and did not attempt landscapes for another year. The results turned out surprisingly like my father's painting. This cannot have been a learnt thing. It must have been inherited. All three subjects too, which interested my father, had the same appeal to me.

Now let us look at my wife. Her parents were landsmen and their parents had apparently been the same. We got a 36 foot East Cornwall lugger and had her fitted as a ketch. We spent the long vacations for ten years having something of a busman's holiday in the Minches. My wife took to it as if she had been born in a Cornish cove. It was astonishing and puzzled many people. Someone said that there must have been a fine old seaman somewhere in her ancestry. There was. We found him in the end. There was not one but two great admirals and she had no idea of this.

It looks as if that vital spark is born with you and handed down to you. It could mean that the mind from which you are projected is compounded of the vital sparks of hundreds of ancestors mixed together and that a selection is sent out with you when you are born. But the admiral's sea-keeping sense would never be given to the descendant of a thousand farmers. It had to be there from remote antiquity and the original brass-bound man was handed it long ago as a very special gift. We are getting very near to the Buddhist's idea of Nirvana; but there is still something missing. There may be a great mingling of personalities somewhere far up the scale of life, yet it will take a very long time before the farmer becomes a seaman.

12 'George', or the Superconscious

We have talked about a considerable number of differing subjects in this short study. Much of it probably does not make sense to those who read it. However, it may be less difficult to those who read psychology and have been told that there is some obscure part of the subconscious mind which often goes by the fancy name of 'George'.

I do not think myself that this part of the human make-up is subconscious. I think that all the evidence goes to show that it is superconscious. To call it 'George' is an insult to something which clearly knows far more than we do in our waking lives. All sorts of nonsense is attributed to George's mischievous tricks with ouija boards and such like. But, if a human mind can be shown to exist on a higher level than the mind on earth, is there any reason to suppose that it might not amuse itself at the expense of minds which did not treat it with proper respect? When approached reasonably this unknown factor of mind is most serious and extremely exact. It is the method of approach which is at fault. If you treat a higher version of yourself as if it were an idiot child, what can you expect but ridicule?

It seems to me, although I am not of course really capable of giving an opinion, that this unknown quality of the mind is really our own self on the next level of the Spiral of Evolution. It knows far more than we do because (its vibrational level being far higher) it does not have to use a brain to filter out everything, except such parts of its experience as are suitable to life on earth. It lives in a timeless zone and can consider everything at leisure. It is far more our real self than we are in bodily life. Time being instantaneous to it, it knows the earthly future of its own projected self. Yet, owing to the fact that each whorl of the spiral extends further out than the one beneath, there is bound to be some distortion when its knowledge is transmitted to the whorl below. This is clear when we draw it out in diagrams.

This part of our mentality appears to live for ever, yet there are at least two higher whorls on the spiral. The one above our own has no rate for death. Somehow the mind appears to move on from the timeless state and re-enter a world where time passes once more. There is no need to bother about this here. Obviously we are not meant to do much about it, for we seem to be here to gather information which can be contemplated higher up. But the spiral shows us a great deal which should be comforting to those who worry about what happens to themselves or their friends when they die.

As I have said, the next whorl of the spiral is larger and extends further out than the one on which we live. Nearly all things which we know here are on it also. Blue is blue and gold is gold. But when people's minds slip up on to the higher level, either by accident or by illness or in sleep, they not infrequently report looking down on their earthly bodies from a height of a few feet above and to one side of them. The spiral explains this completely. Being on the higher whorl, the viewer is both above and to one side of his body. Until he reaches the second whorl, he is in his body. When he is somehow jerked on to the second whorl, he is then higher up and at one side. This is not strange, it is obvious when once you have found the clue.

Divination with the pendulum is one reasonably exact way of learning things about higher levels of vibrations, that is of whorls on the spiral, which are known as planes of living. The pendulum itself is no more than a piece of apparatus. It is not something with a mind of its own, nor magical in any way. It can be nothing more than a lump of chewing gum on a length of cotton. But the operator's mind has control over what the pendulum shall do. It can tell it for instance that it will count ten years for every turn the pendulum makes when tuned in to the 30 inch rate for age and held over a given object. Or the mind can tell it to count one year for each turn and it will apparently do so. This does not mean that the whole operation is mental. As I write this my mind is telling my brain so to control the pen that it will write down such words as I wish it to do. But the pen is the necessary inanimate instrument for the writing. So is the pendulum for this form of divination. With a pendulum you could learn what was happening to a spacecraft on the far side of a planet, as easily as you can find out what is happening to the inside of somebody's body to whom you are linked in Australia. We have done this, checked it and know that it is quite simple. Why it happens is another matter and it needs much practical, scientific study to find out. But don't call your higher mentality 'George'. He may not like it.

13 Only Allah is All-Knowing

We are still finding ancient beliefs, which appear to be correct. Telepathy exists, as hundreds had affirmed it did, and now we appear to find that the mental side of our being owes something to those blood relations of ours who died long ago. There was some sense in it when the Arabs hung the pedigrees of their horses round their beautiful necks.

It seems probable that far too little attention is given to this kind of thing. After all you do not expect a Suffolk Punch to sire the winner of the Grand National; or a poodle and a fox terrier to produce the winning collie at the sheepdog trials. Such things are known to be absurd. Why should man be an exception to this heredity? With sheepdogs at any rate it is mental qualities which you are testing at the trials, as anyone must know who has watched these beautiful animals. Many a time, at anchor in a Highland loch, I have watched three or four dogs bring along hundreds of sheep from a whole rugged mountain face, perhaps two thousand feet high or more, and never miss one amid the gullies and boulders. Don't tell me that this skill is due to environment. It is the result of careful breeding over hundreds of years. The same must be true of human beings and could be studied without too much difficulty.

My wife's boat skill or my attempts at drawing appear to be direct memories from single individuals and nothing to do with a nebulous subhuman part. I think it must have a direct connection with individual minds on a higher and not a lower level. It is superconscious rather than subconscious. Hereditary memory is private to you and not available to humanity at large. I do not really believe that anything of this sort can be the subconscious tribal memories postulated by psychologists. It is too individual for that and there is no apparent distinction between different grades of it.

Of course this could be used as an argument in favour of the theory of reincarnation. It may be your own memory from a former existence that you are tapping. But it does not look as if this is the right answer, because you can get these memories from more than one ancestor. My drawing appears to come from my father but the love of the Hebrides seems to come from my mother's people. These attributes could not have come from a single individual ancestor.

All the way through an investigation of this kind, it is the small indications which we must look for. Slowly they will build up into a great whole.

The Buddhists have their Wheel of Life, which is similar to our compass rose of rates; although they do not seem to have got as far as the spiral. But the general idea seems to be much the same. They believe that the mind goes on developing until it is at last absorbed in the whole of Mind (Nirvana). I think much of this must have been guessing, for it seems unlikely that their thinkers could have risen many whorls in the spiral. Still it does not appear to differ to any great extent from what the pendulum is trying to tell us.

As indifferently explained and comparatively misunderstood in the West, the doctrine of Nirvana does not seem particularly attractive to those with a Christian background. But examined more closely, it seems to make more sense than the celestial concert parties which we were brought up to expect in a future life. The Buddhist quest for Nirvana was a highly developed idea. Life on earth was thought to be an unpleasant experience; but you had to endure it again and again, not necessarily perhaps on the earth whorl, until you improved your mind to such an extent that it could join up with the greater one. Although this is often translated as oblivion, that seems to be a most unlikely answer. The smaller mind is simply joined to a greater one and an increased sense of perfection and bliss could well result from the union as the Buddhists believe; but individuality remains. A few people perhaps may think that their intelligence is perfect but the great majority know its limits and would welcome additions to it. Whatever mind it is that we contact through the pendulum code, it is far more knowledgeable than the one we use every day. Whether the Buddhist Nirvana is far higher still, is, I think, a matter of guessing both for us and for them. However, I can see little at fault in the Buddhist theory as far as we are instructed by the pendulum. It might well be that Christianity would look much the same as Buddhism, if it were stripped of the barnacles of dogma, which have grown on its hull through the ages; but the barnacles have grown so thick that it is hard to see the ship inside.

The Lord Buddha probably never saw the sea and his doctrine, produced far away from it, was bound to be unsatisfactory in some directions. It did not account for the men who moved on what seemed to be a totally alien element. Christian, Moslem and Hebrew all knew the beauty and fear of the ocean. Not so the Buddhist and therefore he was condemned to an almost endless circle of boring lives.

No, there is not enough of the seaman 'chancing his arm' in Buddhism. I have quoted elsewhere the fine remark on this subject in the Orkneyinga Saga. When Sigurd, Earl of Orkney, asked his mother whether he should go to Dublin and fight in the war against the native Irish, she replied: 'I would have raised thee in my wool-chest had I thought that thou shouldst live for ever.' Sigurd went and did not return. But he won an honoured name in the process and perhaps his mother was consoled with that.

My wife once said: 'I can't understand people who are always looking for security. Surely the whole point of life is to learn how to deal with insecurity.' No real artist can ever be secure, for he knows that he can never create a perfect picture. Whatever he does he will see flaws in it. It was for this reason that the Moslems always used to put an error in the weaving of a rug. Allah would not like it to be perfect. Only Allah could make the perfect thing. I like this idea. Many of their ideas are good and their ancient literature shows a sense of humour far in advance of anything in contemporary mediaeval Europe.

Now the only faith you need in order to get to this stage of thinking is a belief that your observations from your own experiments are reasonably accurate. You do not start with somebody's statement that God wishes you to do this or that. You collect observed fact, which appears to tell you what I have written now and from these facts you reason. To this extent you are far nearer to the scientific approach, but the reasoning from what you have observed brings you closer to the faith of the religious people. What is the obvious conclusion that you are likely to draw? Surely it must be that somebody, long ago, worked all this out in a scientific manner and that much religious teaching today is the survival here and there of part of what was once knowledge.

Appendix on Dreams

Future Dreams (I also describe these as Dunne type dreams)

(1) 16 August 1968. On 12 August I wrote to Mrs Beresford and in the course of the letter remarked that I was taking an interest in the Blue Stones (the diorites) of Stonehenge, which Geoffrey of Monmouth had (in the reign of Henry I) ascribed to an origin in Ireland. Archaeologists today believe that they came from Prescelly in south-west Wales, but I knew that there were diorites in Ireland.

On 16 August I had a letter from Mrs Beresford, which began as follows:

5 a.m. 13th August, 1969. I had such an odd dream. I was sitting in a very pleasant room and talking to you. (We have never met, nor, as far as I know, seen photographs of each other.) You had on a white shirt (improbable), open at the neck and either the sleeves rolled up or short ones (correct). I was struck by the pleasant tone of your voice and thought how well it fitted in with the surroundings. We had a small quantity of bits of stone on a piece of felt laid on a small, polished table and you said, 'I still say these came from Ireland' and you went on talking about the bits, but I have lost what was said. The strange thing was that I had no shoes, but a kind of binding round my feet like canvas, which continued over my ankles. I also had very long hair. Altogether, although it was myself, I was not as I am now. I don't know if my face was the same of course, but I seemed to be in fancy dress with a wig, or I suppose it was a wig, I

certainly wasn't dressed for calling. What an odd dream. I've written it down now in case I forget it.

Her letter continues: 'Thursday (14th August). I have just got your letter. How did I pick· up your thoughts about Stonehenge and I was dressed for the part, or what was it?'

Of course this is one of the most remarkable specimens in our collection. Two points are clear at once: (1) Mrs Beresford dreamed about Ireland and the stones ahead of the time at which she got the letter. (2) She somehow obtained information in her dream from the letter, which she had not yet received. It is not known what kind of clothes or footwear were worn in the British Isles about 4,000 years ago. What is known is that I never wear white shirts now and have not done so for years. There is always something slightly wrong in these dreams.

One point is worth noting concerning Mrs Beresford's dress in her dream: although there is no reason to suppose that she had somehow discovered the correct garments of so long ago, it does seem evident that she must have been actually thinking about them while asleep and imagined herself dressed in what she then believed to be right. This is not a memory impression, past or future, but a piece of real thinking. In the next dream, which is one of mine, the same kind of thing happened. I dreamed about a particular type of boat and that I was aboard it. Two days later I was sent a picture of the same type of boat, but the view was from a distance and I was not on board.

(2) 16 February 1970. Woke with a very detailed picture of the poop deck of a small wooden ship. She had no rail or bulwark. The vessel was new and I understood her to be a fishing boat of perhaps fifteen tons. She was built of reddish wood, which I thought must be cedar. I took her to be some Arab vessel of dhow type and understood that something was called a taku or tākle, but that was all I got from a man leaning in the hold, or fish well, opposite me on the port side. The man was about forty with a roundish face, which was not very dark. I took him to be the master of the vessel, who was sailing her a short distance across a sheet of calm water, perhaps a harbour or estuary, presumably to complete her fitting out. The boat

was evidently on the port tack and heeled over to starboard. The man had on a long dirty white garment and a turban of the same colour. I could not see the tiller or helmsman.

There seemed to be no possible cause for me to have dreamed about a dhow or about an arab.

Two days later I received a postcard from a friend in East Africa. It was sent from Lake Naivasha on 2 February. On the front was a reproduction in colour of a painting of a dhow of about the size of the one in my dream. She was on the same tack and apparently built of unpainted reddish wood. On board were three men in white garments and two in dark ones. There were two shrouds on either side of the mast. These were not set up with dead-eyes, or rigging screws, as one would have expected in Europe, but with blocks and purchases, which I would have spoken of as tackles and pronounced tākle with a long a. There were no bulwarks except in the eyes of the boat and their places were taken by wicker work screens.

This postcard was evidently the exciting cause of my dream, but whether it was in future time or came to me by telepathy is not so clear. Presumably telepathy is ruled out, because it was sent four days before I got it. This is less important than the differences between the dream and the picture. In the dream, I was aboard the boat and she was sailing. In the postcard she was sailing towards me and some appreciable way off. It seems clear that I saw the postcard two days before I got it; thought about what I saw; noticed on what tack she was sailing, that at least one man was dressed in white and that it was calm water. Then I must have imagined myself on board.

From this we can deduce a most important fact. A person on the second mental level can evidently think and imagine things just as he does on the earth level. Since the second level is beyond sleep and death, a person is clearly able to think and imagine things after he has died. This may well seem to be the most important dream in the whole collection. In whatever manner the picture came into my mind, I certainly thought about it on the second mental level and made up a new picture from it on that level.

Clearly this is by no means unusual. Mrs Beresford was also seeing, thinking and imagining on the second level. It is only as we get used to handling the material that we begin to see how much of vast importance is to be learnt from this study.

(3) 13 March 1970. I woke at 6.30 hot and damp. Mina was still fast asleep. I got out of bed and went to the chair near the end of her bed on which were my day clothes and her long dressing gown. I pulled off my damp things and, knowing that she would soon need it, put her dressing gown on her feet, before pulling on a dry day shirt. At once, and without waking up, she called in an urgent voice: 'Take the things off my feet.' I was struggling into my shirt in the dark. She repeated the call. I snatched the dressing gown off her feet. It is lighter than my shirt (being 1 lb 2 oz.); in fact it seemed almost weightless. She called out a third time before I could get my shirt on. I got back to bed and waited till she woke up a quarter of an hour later. Then she told me that in her sleep she had felt a considerable weight being put on her feet and thought it was all my day clothes with several heavy things in the pockets (my knife alone weighs half a pound).

The importance of this lies in the sensation of weight. When she woke fully, my wife tested in bed the feeling of the dressing gown on her toes. She could just tell that there was something there. Asleep, that something was heavy and uncomfortable. If, as I think, there is a difference of four times in the rate of vibration between the two mental levels, the abnormality experienced in the weight is explained. On the verge of waking, my wife suddenly felt something weighing 4½ lbs put on her feet, because her mind was really on the second level and the object was on the earth one.

This type of experience has often been recorded in ghost stories and the whole thing could easily be tested with sleeping persons; yet I feel reasonably certain that this is the correct explanation.

(4) 5 November 1968. Woke about 6 a.m. and while waking appeared to notice a loud hum and the arrival of a very large beetle in the light above the bedside lamp (of course this light was not on at the time). The beetle appeared so large when seen from below that I seemed to think that it must be a stag beetle (*Lucanus cervus*). Immediately I appeared to be looking down on it from above. The wing-cases were closed, which would not

have been so had it been really flying. I could see the ridges on them and they were not as smooth as with *Lucanus*. Their colour was a dull olive-green and not brown.

A few minutes later I really woke up. Presently, my wife woke too and we talked a little. At 7 a.m. we listened to the News. Soon after, a large blue-fly hit my head with a loud buzz. It roared round the light several times, fell into the tea cups and was a general nuisance.

I had spent quite a lot of thought and time observing beetles flying at the cone of the light, a month or so before the dream occurred. But the dream seems to have been triggered off by the behaviour of a blue-fly an hour after the dream was observed. The future appearance of the fly was the inciting cause. This is exactly what was noticed by Dunne in his much more exciting dreams and led him to posutlate that some dreams are compounded of past and future memories.

(5) 8 November 1968. As I was waking about 6 a.m. a picture in full colour suddenly appeared. It resembled a postcard in proportion of length to breadth and was certainly rectangular, although blurred at the edges. The picture showed the black

Figure 7   Rough sketch from memory of an unknown old steamship seen in postcard colours in dream 5. The actual picture was wider than I have drawn it and was postcard shape. The vessel may have been rather larger.

painted hull of a coal-burning steamship. She was clearly a passenger vessel with white upperworks. She was lying made fast to a stone jetty, which ran almost across the middle of the picture at a slight angle. The vessel was an old one with a straight stem and high thin funnel amidships. The funnel had a black band above and the rest was red. There were two tall post masts fore and aft. She had probably been built sixty years ago. She appeared to be a British mail packet and not an ocean-going liner. The whole thing gave the impression of being the projection of a coloured postcard.

We listened to the 7 a.m. News. In this it was stated that the old Queen Elizabeth was being withdrawn from service after thirty years and that the Commodore of the Line was taking her on her last cruise. The Queen Mother, who had launched her, had just been to look over her at Southampton (Figure 7).

I think that the key to this dream is the red and black funnel. I was shown an old ship with the red and black colours of the Royal Mail. This was a Dunne type dream combining both past and future memories and neither were quite correctly linked.

(6) 8 November 1968. Woke for a short time during the night and, while dropping off again, the face of an elderly man appeared for an instant. It was seen side view and looking to my left. I did not know the face, which was in black and white and appeared to be an engraving. It could have been on a continental postage stamp, or on something of that kind.

Two months later (10 January 1969) I happened to handle and look at a Yugoslav postage stamp depicting Tito's head. It appeared similar in all respects to the picture in this dream.

(7) 8 November 1968. Dream from Mrs V. Beresford. Extract from her letter, which arrived that day:

> On 16th April this year I wrote in my diary—and told Miss Plant about it in the morning—I had a dreadful dream. I saw the whole side of a block of buildings collapse. I saw the furniture hurled down and people screamed in terror; the dust was thick as smoke, I heard someone say: 'Collapsed like a pack of cards.' Now as I say I told Miss Plant in the morning (she will bear me out in this). Exactly a month later the block of flats at Ronans Point [actually Ronan Point]

went and the headlines were: 'Collapsed like a pack of cards', said an onlooker. Now in some way I was able to reach up and grab a bit of the future, but why me, I had no one there, and I knew no one connected with it.

This is a perfect example of a Dunne future memory dream.

Figure 8 Rough sketch from memory of dream 8.

His dreams of fires and earthquakes were just like this. They were derived from reading newspapers and even contained misprints which were in the papers. Mrs Beresford's dream was experienced a month before the building collapsed.

(8) 13 November 1968. Very stormy night. Woke hot and uncomfortable at 2.15 a.m. realising that there was a great deal of fuss and bother going on. I saw nobody and heard no voices but understood that something had to be got into a church before somebody arrived. Then I saw the picture of the inside of a building with high, plain Gothic arches. The end one of these was partially illuminated, the rest on all sides rose vaguely into darkness. There was an area of light at the foot of the visible arch and in the middle of my picture. On this appeared something, which looked like a large rectangular black box illuminated on the far side. It was set diagonally to the two feet of the arch. This was clearly an artist's impression of something and looked as if a black and white drawing had been done in pencil and wash (Figure 8)

I went to sleep again soon, having attempted to fix all this in my memory. The fuss was still apparently going on and a second picture appeared. It was in very pale colours. Most of it was taken up with the figure of a young man in voluminous white garments. His face was far too regular to be that of a living person. I realised that I was looking at an artist's idealised drawing. The face was of a fair northern type and it was smiling. I could not see the hair. Behind him on his left and partly hidden by his clothes was a large jar, as big as a carboy and much the same shape. It was not unlike a late Roman amphora. It was a very pale pink and round it horizontally ran three broad bands of very pale cobalt blue. I rather think there were other jars on the far side of the figure, but they were less distinct. At first I took this to be an advertisement of a pottery, or something of that kind. The drawing was good but the whole picture was rather anaemic. It might have been done at the end of the nineteenth century.

I did not think that the dreams could possibly have come from my memories, yet the origins of the two pictures seemed to be clear. This was only two days after Armistice Day.

There had been more in the news about this than usual, for it was the fiftieth anniversary of the end of the First World War. I had little doubt that the first picture was somebody's memory of an artist's impression of the tomb of the Unknown Warrior in Westminster Abbey. The thing I had taken for a black box was the tomb itself, open in the floor with light on one side.

This was not all. The day before my dream Bert my gardener had to leave in the morning for the funeral of his sister-in-law in Beer. She had died in hospital. The funeral was all arranged and then there was a hitch. The death certificate had not been made out properly. The whole thing was held up for a couple of days.

Here surely was the background of fuss and waiting in my dream. It seemed most probable that I had been getting it telepathically from Bert, who is most sensitive and easily upset by worries of this kind. I asked him this morning if he had slept well. No, the gales and other things had kept him wakeful for much of the night.

The second picture, still with the background of fuss, now seemed easier to interpret. Surely it was a late Victorian picture of Jesus turning the water into wine. It was in the delicate colours of which I know Bert is very fond. During the service probably Bert had remembered some picture seen and enjoyed in his childhood. He observes well.

(9) 18 November 1968. I had a letter from Colin Franklin dated 14 November 1968. In this he said:

I stupidly did not have a pencil by me last night, but record clearly a moonlight bathing and then in the middle of it near some bathing hut I looked back and saw the huge hotel building with smoke, far too much of it, coming out of the chimneys. I began to realise it was on fire and suggested to my companions that we must go straight back there. I had clear doubts and wonderings about dashing upstairs and finding my family and that is all I can recall, although now (still before eleven in the morning) I can see the uncommonly solid Edwardian hotel building, rectangular, very high, lots of chimneys, very large and I wonder where the tragedy is going to happen, or did happen. Nothing to do with me so far.

Now this is absolutely clear. The letter was written on 14 November. Colin had no idea what caused his dream. In the 7 a.m. news of 17 November we were told about the tragic fire in a Brighton Hotel in which seven people died. On the television news that evening the building was shown and corresponded in a remarkable way to that which he had described. It would hardly be possible to have a clearer case of event preceding cause. This is the second dramatic one we have reported. In the dream state the time sequence can be utterly, completely and dramatically reversed. Dunne showed it long ago; but few took any notice except to try to demonstrate that his mathematics, which had nothing to do with his observed facts, might be incorrect.

Mrs Beresford's dream of the Ronan Point collapse and Colin Franklin's one of the Brighton Hotel fire were not only in future time but they can only have come to them either from TV or the newspapers. They were not really connected with the dreamers at all. I have already published in *A Step in the Dark* something which is stranger still. I must tell the story again for somewhere in it there must be an important clue.

(10) In May 1964 it had been arranged for me to give a little TV demonstration on dowsing here. It was to be produced later at Bristol. John Irving, the producer, and his cameraman were due here at Hole at 11 o'clock. At about this time a car drew up outside and I went down expecting to see the producer. Instead I found a completely unknown young man. As I reached the car, he climbed out looking a little dazed. 'I feel odd', he said. This was rather a jolt, for if he had food poisoning or something of that kind, it would have been difficult to deal with it there. Instead of asking if he were ill, something made me say: 'You aren't going to tell me that you have been here before?'

Not knowing what he normally looked like, I cannot say that he looked pale, or startled, but I think that he did both. 'Oh yes,' he said. 'Are there some other buildings behind the house, that I can't see?' 'Yes indeed', I replied. 'There is a kind of court behind.' He asked if he might see it and I told him to go and look at anything he liked. So I went with the young man, who was the cameraman called Graham Tidman, and we walked past the east end of the house. He looked at the garden wall, which I had found completely rotten and had had to rebuild and reshape. 'It used not to be like that', he said. 'There used to be buildings against that wall.' I told him that I had heard that there were pig-sties and cowsheds there at one time.

We walked round into the court. He looked at it carefully. 'Yes', he said. 'This is just as it was in my dreams.' Mind you I had never seen this man before and only assumed that he was John Irving's cameraman. We returned to the east side of the house and looked at the walls and the little herb garden I had made for my wife. 'There were buildings here', he said. 'They were pulling them down and someone said: "Now we will be able to see the sea." ' I told him this would have been true. We could see a tiny wedge of sea, like something seen over the backsight of a rifle, but it was very small. The trees in the distance had evidently grown since the time the man was talking about.

Mr Tidman next said that there ought to be a nursery garden over there outside the gate, on the left side sloping down the hill. I took him to look. On moving to Hole, we had found an uncultivated wilderness, but we had slowly turned it into a kitchen garden again. He looked over the wall in a kind of daze. 'Yes, that is right', he said. 'I can't understand it. I have never been here before and nowhere near it; but this is exactly as I saw it in my dream and I have had that dream five times.'

Graham Tidman said that he had never been within miles of Hole and no known friend or relative had been there either. He had never heard what it once looked like and he had no idea what to expect when he did arrive there. It hit him as a shock and he felt 'odd'.

We knew various things about the house and we know more now than we did at that time. Most of the Tudor building is as it was several hundred years ago. There had been pig-sties and cattle sheds where Mr Tidman had seen them. They are on a plan attached to a deed of 1896. A new roof had been put on the house and a date of 1929 is scratched on the plaster in the masonry of a chimney in the roof space. It appears that what Mr Tidman saw going on in his dream actually took place when he was either unborn, or so young that he could not possibly have known anything about it.

Apparently, the only link between the dreamer and the house had occurred not only after he had had the dreams but his whole lifetime after the happenings which he had dreamed about. There is no way of evading this. Since there was apparently no human link, the only one available is the house itself. In his dreams, it seems he must have picked up words and incidents fixed in the stonework of the building. This would be wildly improbable had we had no previous experience of these strange things and we will not elaborate on it now. This is just to fix the point in the reader's mind.

There have been attempts to explain this knowledge of 'I have seen all this already' as a slipping of the mind. A kind of missing a beat so to speak. That does not explain how it can possibly happen. Yet all through this we begin to see that there is a mental zone in which time does not run in the sequence we are accustomed to.

(11) November 1968. Saw a large wheel with many spokes and apparently the dark underside of the vehicle to which it belonged. There was no colour. Although the wheel looked like a carriage wheel, it stood on one of a pair of light railway tracks. I heard a voice say, '. . . should the train push'. I felt that they ought to put a chock under the wheel (Figure 9A).

In the afternoon I was reading the Sunday papers. On a page in the *Observer* was a large photograph of a man on an ancient

Figure 9 Two sketches: A. From memory of dream 11 experienced at about 11.45 p.m., 23 November 1968. B. Man riding a boneshaker bicycle, from a photograph seen 4 p.m. in the *Observer*, 24 November.

boneshaker bicycle riding in a town street against a background of pavement and pillared portico. His feet, right over the axle of the big front wheel, had to drive the thing along by main force (Figure 9B). One can see at once, comparing these two sketches, that this was the origin of my wheel dream of about twelve hours earlier. Here we find a most interesting sequence of errors and, by a great piece of luck, I think we can see why they happened.

My ordinary mind waking up appeared to hear '. . . should the train push'. From this it assumed that it was looking at an old-fashioned train and even thought that something must be done to stop the train pushing. Since it was a train, it displaced the edge of the pavement and the shadows of the wheels and turned these into railway tracks. As only a fraction of the photograph was visible, the man's legs and parts of his body and coat were interpreted as the underside of a railway carriage. The curious diagonal bracing of the bicycle's wheel was turned into the radial spokes of a normal wheel and so the waking memory registered and remembered the underside of a railway carriage. Some other part of my mind (or somebody else's mind) had observed the difficulty the rider was having in turning the wheel with his feet and remarked something like: 'It would be a strain to push.' It is completely rational if you can spot the clue.

(12) 14 September 1969. I woke at 5.20 a.m. In front of me was a group of people, none of whom was known to me. They were in a large building with girders and other objects, which I did not observe correctly. There was an arched window in the end wall. Apparently the people were discussing some performance, which they had just seen and a man's voice said: 'Did you understand a word of the last bit?' The man's face was indistinct. The women appeared smartly dressed. They might have been standing on stairs or a gangway with solid sides. The group was in the position which I have roughly sketched (Figure 10).

About midday we returned from Seaton with the Sunday papers. In the *Sunday Times,* which I read before lunch, was a picture of Colin Davis, Conductor of the BBC Symphony Orchestra, autographing the hat of a girl who was waiting for

Figure 10 Rough sketch from memory of a dream experienced in the early morning of 14 September 1969.

admission to the last night of the proms. I have sketched the top part of this photograph (Figure 11). It will be obvious how similar the grouping is and the arched window was in fact a doorway. There is an extra, fair-haired girl in the dream picture, but she is in reality a badly observed portion of another woman's dress.

There was an interval of seven hours between the time of the dream and the actual seeing of the picture. This is a Dunne type

Figure 11 Rough sketch of a photograph printed in the *Sunday Times* and observed at midday on the same day, seven hours later.

of future memory. It shows how many dreams are built up on rapid glances at newspapers or television pictures and how the next level of mind apparently reasons (to some extent incorrectly) from what the earth-level counterpart is going to see.

Flash Dreams

(13) 6 November 1968. For a brief instant before dropping off to sleep, two male faces appeared side by side. They were youngish men, tidy and clean shaven. I had no knowledge of seeing them before, although they were visible in considerable detail. Both had light-brown hair. The one on my right might have been forty years old and had a short face with a pointed

chin. The other appeared to be a little younger with an oval, well filled out face. The first one faded instantly. The other lingered and faded slowly becoming translucent and reversed like a photographic negative. Both had appeared full face to me, but were not looking at me. One would have thought that they stood about five yards away and were engaged in conversation.

(I have often seen faces of this kind before, and always when just dropping off to sleep. They have been of both sexes and never anybody I knew by sight. Others have reported having had similar dreams. These pictures could hardly have been conjured up in one's mind. They are definite portraits in detail of particular individuals and not stylised figures conjured up in the imagination. It will be observed that while pictures of this kind always seem to happen when we are just going to sleep, other incidents take place when we are waking up.)

(14) 7 November 1968. Instant flash when going to sleep. Picture of a young woman, about half length, standing and turned partly to the right. She was against a dark background with no visible features. It was purplish brown. The woman was about thirty. She had a round, rosy face and rather prominent teeth. She was laughing. Her hair was short, waved and reddish-brown and she wore a white dress. She was unknown to me, but would undoubtedly have been recognisable to somebody who did know her. The whole thing was like an instant glimpse of a coloured snapshot.

(15) 8 November 1968. While dropping off to sleep, a man's face appeared for an instant. Unlike the two previous cases it was not central but appeared in the left-hand bottom corner of my field of vision. In fact part of the side of the face was not visible on my 'screen' at all. It showed for so short a time that I was unable to get much detail. Seen full face it was a young man with a pointed chin. The background was an indistinct purplish brown. It was exactly as if someone had put on a slide incorrectly in a projector.

(16) 9 November 1968. I saw a flash of colour of a white area with two large packets of cigarettes in it. They had brown bands and lettering on white. There was also a small black object wrapped in cellophane, which might have been a pipe.

This was completely detailed but of short duration. (I do not smoke.)

(17) 14 November 1968. I woke at 7.00 a.m. Something seemed to be going on; but it did not register. Then I saw a picture of a beach. This was viewed across the sea at a distance of about half a mile. The beach was of yellowish sand and curved round to a low point on my left. There were three or more human figures visible near the left end of the sand and half-way up its slope. There were no cliffs. The beach simply rose to low, pointed, light-green hills. The picture could well have been a coloured advertisement of some foreign place. There were no houses in it.

(18) 22 November 1968. Saw an indistinct picture of a brownish cat in what appeared to be a sunlit grassy patch in a wood. The grass was streaked with shadow. The cat lay down and rolled with its legs high in the air.

(19) 3 December 1968. Saw a still in colour. It looked like an old print or perhaps a watercolour painting. There was a broad, slow river in the foreground right across the picture. Beyond this was a yellowish straight road with a number of small figures on it. Some were dressed in bright red or green. Behind the road stood a line of flat-roofed buildings several storeys high. Each was in its separate enclosure. The impression I got from this was that it was a picture of the administrative buildings of a place in India at least a hundred years ago. However, this is only a guess.

(20) 5 December 1968. Somebody threw down an object looking like a roll of cloth on to a window sill. A huge cloud of dust rose in the sunlight coming from the window behind.

(21) 9 December 1968. I saw a flash of two brown puppies. I appeared to be standing up and they seemed to be sitting on my left foot. They had smooth heads and drooping ears. One was more brindled than the other, which was chestnut in colour. I did not see their faces. Their bodies were woolly.

(22) 10 December 1968. Saw a flash of the head and shoulders of an unknown woman. It was in rather pale colour against a whitish background. It was possibly a painting. The woman was three-quarter face to me and looked to be between fifty and sixty. Her hair was rather high on her head.

(23) 13 December 1968. Saw a flash picture of the head and

shoulders of a youngish man full face. There was no colour and the original appeared to be an old-fashioned type of photograph. The man was not attractive. He had a wolfish grin showing his teeth and a dark moustache, which ended in points and may have been waxed. His coat was cut high in front and could have dated shortly before 1914. The whole flash was so rapid that I am surprised at the amount of detail which was registered in my mind.

(24) 16 December 1968. I had a flash dream of a large picture of the head and shoulders of a young woman seen nearly full face. She was dressed in pink with a big brimmed hat of the same colour, which had a pink feather curved over the front of it. The background was pinkish white. Her face was a broad oval with brown eyes and hair. She was pretty but did not appear quite natural. I should think this was a picture from a magazine cover. I should guess the date to have been about 1916.

(25) 22 January 1969. A flash of the grinning face of a small boy. He had a round face and fair hair against a white background. He was about eight years old. The grin was slightly sinister. The child was up to mischief. I did not recognise him.

(26) 29 January 1969. Woke to see an enlarged picture in colour of the foremast of the French prisoner model of a '74' on the hall mantelpiece. It was showing through tall birch trees. A line was attached to the fore topgallant mast and I knew that there was a fish on the end of it. I expected the mast to bend like a trout rod and play the fish. Instead of this the whole mast collapsed and vanished.

(I can think of no explanation for this dream. I see the model every day and, although the rigging needs renewing, it does not bother me.)

(27) 13 July 1969. Flash of four people facing me, standing in line. Three were indistinct. The fourth, on my left in the line, was a thickset woman in a dark-blue dress. She had a stolid looking, dark, heavy face and black hair. She looked bored and unfriendly. I did not know her. This flash might easily have originated in a photograph of an unknown group of people posed for it.

(Like so many of, if not all, the flash type of dream, the

persons in it were evidently not connected with the dreamer. It is remarkable how the people seen in them are never friends or relations. They are all unknown to me. I cannot be certain of course that I have never glanced at pictures of the people involved, but I have no memory of having done so. Each person has character and individuality. They are not imaginary, but pictures of real people in a real setting. There is clearly some important point to be grasped here, although at present it eludes me.)

Reversed Dreams

(28) 27 July 1969. A letter arrived from V. Beresford written on 23 July. I report her dream in her own words:

> Last night I had a very peculiar dream, one of those back to front ones. I saw Mrs R. and her husband come backwards from the door. Open the garage door and drive the car backwards down the lane. But the queer thing was that it seemed as if someone knew it was in wrongly, for the car appeared again coming up the lane through the gate and it all happened in the right sequence. I woke up saying, 'Now that's a funny thing to happen.' There was no sense in such a dream, but it was exactly like a film run back to front.

(29) 9 September 1969. Mrs Beresford wrote again reporting a reversed dream:

> I had the queerest dream last night. Macabre too. I saw a coffin being carried. It was made of (I think) deal and very badly varnished a dreadful, red-brown colour, and abnormally long. What added to the bizarre effect was that the bearers wore rough working clothes and caps on the backs of their heads and were trotting along at a brisk pace, *backwards,* along a country lane. One man said in an exaggerated 'Oxford' voice: 'Burnt be to enough good woods any.' I woke with this in my ear and couldn't make sense of it, till I realised he was also speaking backwards. An odd, senseless kind of dream, but odd that I should hear about the inquest on your brother-in-law by this morning's post.

It was odd indeed. The inquest was followed by cremation three days later.

Not only is the action in the dream reversed; but so are the words spoken by the man reversed in position. 'Any wood is good enough to be burnt' is turned back to front. Yet the letters are not reversed. One would have expected the remark to look like this: tnrub eb ot hguone doog si doow yna. Had this happened Mrs Beresford could not have understood the sounds at all. But you do not hear the sounds of words as letters and it is simply the order of the sequence which is reversed. Had the men or the coffin been completely reversed, no one could possibly have known what they were looking at. The reversal then concerns the order of events and not the constituents of those events.

The only other reversed dream of note is my one about the cat, which I have already quoted.

Erotic Dreams

(Having remarked earlier that I seldom, if ever, had a dream which could be classed as erotic, I awoke to one which could certainly be taken as such.)

(30) On 2 March 1969 I found myself sitting naked beside a large bed in a room with a number of people in front of a wide window on the far side of it. Feeling rather conspicuous, if not exactly embarrassed, I jumped into the bed and pulled the clothes up. I had hardly got settled in it, when a youngish woman also without clothes jumped in too. We were pleased to be together in a friendly but not emotional way and gave each other a hug. The room then began to fade and fill up with a large number of people noisily pushing and jostling. Not liking them much, we stayed quietly in bed. I could see my companion's face in profile. It was nobody I recognised. She was fair and pleasant looking, with rather a long straight nose. She might have been about thirty and a cheerful person with little regard for unnecessary decorum.

The whole of this seemed to take a long time. There was nothing instantaneous about it. The scene changed. I got separated from my girl friend by a crowd of people. However, she returned to me again and we huddled down, amid a large number of people, beneath blankets on some kind of a slope. She remarked to me: 'The Baptist minister's daughter is very shocked by us.' I realised which person was the Baptist minister's daughter. She was a tow-headed and rather sharp-featured woman lying between two others, a few yards to our left. Then it all vanished.

It left me with the impression of having found a friend in time of need. As I became conscious, I realised that some part of my mind had been eagerly attempting to rationalise an almost platonic situation as a physical love affair. This suggests that the real dream takes place at a distinct mental level above that of the waking mind.

I was at a loss to see where this dream could have come from, till I remembered that some days before I had been sent the *Sunday Times* colour supplement of 16 February so I could read some articles on dreams published in it. One full page illustration in this copy was of a painting by Paul Delvaux. It showed a moonlit street, paved and flanked by classical buildings. In file at intervals down the street, stood three nude, fair-haired women. The picture was described as a 'Dream of Sexual Nostalgia'. I think this picture could perhaps have originated the dream of my naked companion, but I am by no means certain of this. There was far more character in the face of my dream friend and I did not see much of her anatomy; although I could feel her back with my hand.

It is to be noticed that three senses are involved here: sight, sound and touch. Many dreams only make use of one, sight or hearing. It is rarer for there to be two, sight and hearing. This is the only one as yet in which I have observed three and have been in definite contact with another person. She felt firm and muscular, unlike the women in the Delvaux painting, who appear somewhat soft and flabby.

(31) 21 March 1969. I dreamt I was sketching in some sand dunes when a naked young woman, with a but slightly developed figure, came up in great distress and said that somebody had stolen her clothes. She was not at all distinct but I felt that something must be done to relieve her anxiety. I

thought that if I tied a pair of my large handkerchiefs together they, with perhaps the addition of my tie, would make a pair of knickers. The rest I felt could be covered by my coat or shirt. I remember telling her to wait until I had spent a few moments in completing my sketch.

Three days later, on 24 March, I was sent a copy of *Britain in the Roman Empire*. On the cover jacket of this book is a photograph of a statuette, presumed to be of Venus, with a huge bow tied between her legs. Her bust is not at all conspicuously formed (Figure 12). This is really a Dunne dream and its significance is not in any way erotic. It simply

Figure 12 Rough sketch from a photograph of a statuette of Venus shown on the jacket of Miss Joan Liversidge's book *Britain in the Roman Empire*. This book reached me three days after I experienced dream 31, which this photograph apparently originated.

indicates surprise and interest in the present of a book, three days before it arrived. The sand dune part of the dream can also be explained. We were hoping to go to Cornwall shortly, to a place where there are sand dunes.

Induced Telepathic Dreams Apparently Unconnected with Dreamer

(These dreams have been published in *Ghost and Ghoul* so I will

Figure 13   Rough sketch from memory of the final incident in dream 32. (I have not looked up contemporary photographs of cars.) Note observer's viewpoint slightly above car, as in numerous reports of 'out of the body' experiences.

give a shortened version of them here.)

(32) The first one of these occurred in Cambridge in 1957. I seemed to be in a car, which was being driven over flat country towards a wide river. This was spanned by a very long iron bridge. It was not unlike an Essex scene. The water was grey and muddy with a strong flow from my left to right. I felt I was looking north. In the first scene the car was approaching the bridge, but about a hundred yards from it.

The scene ended abruptly. Instantly the car was at the abutment of the bridge and was being turned round. The car approached the left side of the bridge then the shot ended.

Next the car had evidently been backed and was coming forward again on the other lock. Below the bridge I could now see a steep slope with a drop of seventy-five feet to the water. My viewpoint was now a few feet above the left side of the car, which was an open one and very old and battered (Figure 13). I was not in it at all. On the left sat a little old man with a sharp face.

I noted, entirely without emotion, that the front of the car was already over the edge of the drop into the water. At this moment the driver (whom I had not noticed before) rose to his feet. He was a burly man in dark clothes and a light-coloured cloth cap. He remarked: 'We'll be dead men any time now, gents.' That was all.

(Now this dream seems to have had no connection with me at all. I can see no reason why I should have dreamed it. I did not know the people or the place. As far as I know I had never read a description of this particular incident in a newspaper. Whatever happened must have taken place about thirty years before I dreamed it. I can only think that it was somebody else's memory communicated to me telepathically, probably by some totally unknown person.)

(33) 5 February 1960. I had almost woken up when I dozed off again.

At once I seemed to be looking out of an upstairs window in a house I did not know. The window was either on a stairway or a landing. It was a tall, sash one, not exactly a bay window, but a wedge-shaped affair with two lights. It projected over a road, or drive, and was painted a light cream colour. The road passed beneath me and out of sight behind. On the left side of my view was the creamy-white stuccoed wall of the house. It appeared to be late Georgian or early Victorian. I had a feeling that the sea was close to the house on the other side. I never saw it, but knew it was there. My mind told me that the house was on a ledge of the cliff above the sea. The scene could have been

Figure 14   Rough sketch from memory of figure with basket seen in dream 33.

somewhere on the south coast of England; although the unusual shape of the window made this doubtful.

Coming down the road towards me was a man in uniform. He was extremely smartly turned out. His ivy-green greatcoat was beautifully cut and flared out a little at the knees. He was slight and not very tall. He appeared to be smoking a small cigar. In the crook of his arm he carried a curious basket. It was oval and of dark brown wicker work, perhaps about eighteen inches long. The man himself had an extremely nice, friendly face. I took him to be a British officer, who had served a long time in a hot climate. The picture stopped dead when he was still sauntering down the road towards me and was perhaps fifteen yards away (Figure 14).

The next shot came on in another room, facing the opposite way. Although apparently a bedroom, it was bare of furniture, but someone else was in it with me. I knew that the officer was in the house and about to come into the room. Outside the door I heard him say to himself: 'What a beast of a basket! I suppose this is for English.' There the dream ended.

(The first strange thing about this is that it could not have been a memory from a living person. The date must have been about a hundred years or more before I had this dream. Had any living person remembered the scene he would have been in the region of 110 years old at least. We can safely rule out 'living memory' from this story.

Then some two years after *Ghost and Ghoul* was published, I had a letter from a lady overseas, which explained part of the mystery. She knew what 'English' was. It was a kind of spin put on the ball, in a Spanish form of the game of Fives, by using an odd-shaped basket. Now how are we going to explain this quite amazing series of events? I dream of something, which must have happened long ago in the nineteenth century, which includes something in a game about which I knew nothing. It is inconceivable that such an elaborate picture could be built up in the imagination. Apparently I have picked up two most elaborate scenes, which obviously had happened to other people many years ago. These dreams are impossible by ordinary earth standards. So indeed are many of our less spectacular dreams.)

Scraps of Conversation without Pictures

It appears that dreams with voices in them are seldom the experiences of the dreamer (past or future) but are picked up in some unexplained way from other people. They may be their memories, or they may be things leaking from television or sound radio. It is too early yet to come to any conclusion. The problem of dreaming already shows parallels with that of seeing and hearing ghosts. In both groups of experience one appears to be dealing with forms of natural projection of what might be called thought images. In both there is much evidence of a distortion of the time scale. It should be easier nowadays (when everyone is familiar with television) to see the possibilities. What one seems to be observing is natural television without the aid of machines, and this applies to each group of phenomena. With each group (dream and ghost) there is the same distortion of the earthly time factor. You can receive impressions of both future and past projections. This is where the major problem seems to lie. Telepathy (that is thought projection from one person to another) is already widely accepted as fact. Now we have to accept pictorial projection and audible projection as well. It is far more difficult to see how any of these can take place in future time. Dreams apparently show that this can take place, at least that is how it appears from the scanty evidence which we have collected so far and which was made quite clear in Dunne's observations.

Here are a few examples of scraps of conversation heard while asleep:

(34) 15 November 1968. Woke through a confused murmur of voices. All I could distinguish was somebody saying: 'She eats dry eggs.' Presumably this should have been 'dried' eggs. (I certainly haven't discussed anyone eating dried eggs. It sounds a revolting sort of vice; but was probably in reality part of a perfectly normal discussion between two women on house-keeping matters.)

(35) 23 November 1968. Woke to hear someone blaming Melchior Rousseau, or Roussel, for something I could not catch.

(36) I heard a buzz of conversation, apparently between two women. The only phrase which I managed to catch was: 'Do you take small boats?'

(37) I saw what I took to be Mina and asked: 'What are you going to do?' She replied: 'I've got a new book now.' The figure was extremely hazy. It may not have been Mina at all.

(38) Mina heard a scrap of conversation from some unknown man. 'I don't want to spoil my wife but what shall I give her for Christmas?' This appears to have no relation to either of us.

(39) 15 December 1968. Woke apparently hearing Mina saying: 'He's just begun to read a publication now.' It may not have been my wife and she was certainly asleep at the time.

Shock Dreams

(40) At about midnight Mina had woken up with a great jump. A black ball had flown at her and missed. It was followed by an orange ball, which hit her head and was hot. She thought she had had a stroke and was relieved to find she had not. This dream was apparently set off by the pressure of internal wind.

At one time she used to have a lot of these jumps. Once in Scotland she had a tremendous one. I asked her what had happened. She replied (though still asleep) that someone had thrown a ball at her. On another occasion she said she had fallen down a step.